21

SILBER
TRIENNALE

SILVER
TRIENNIAL

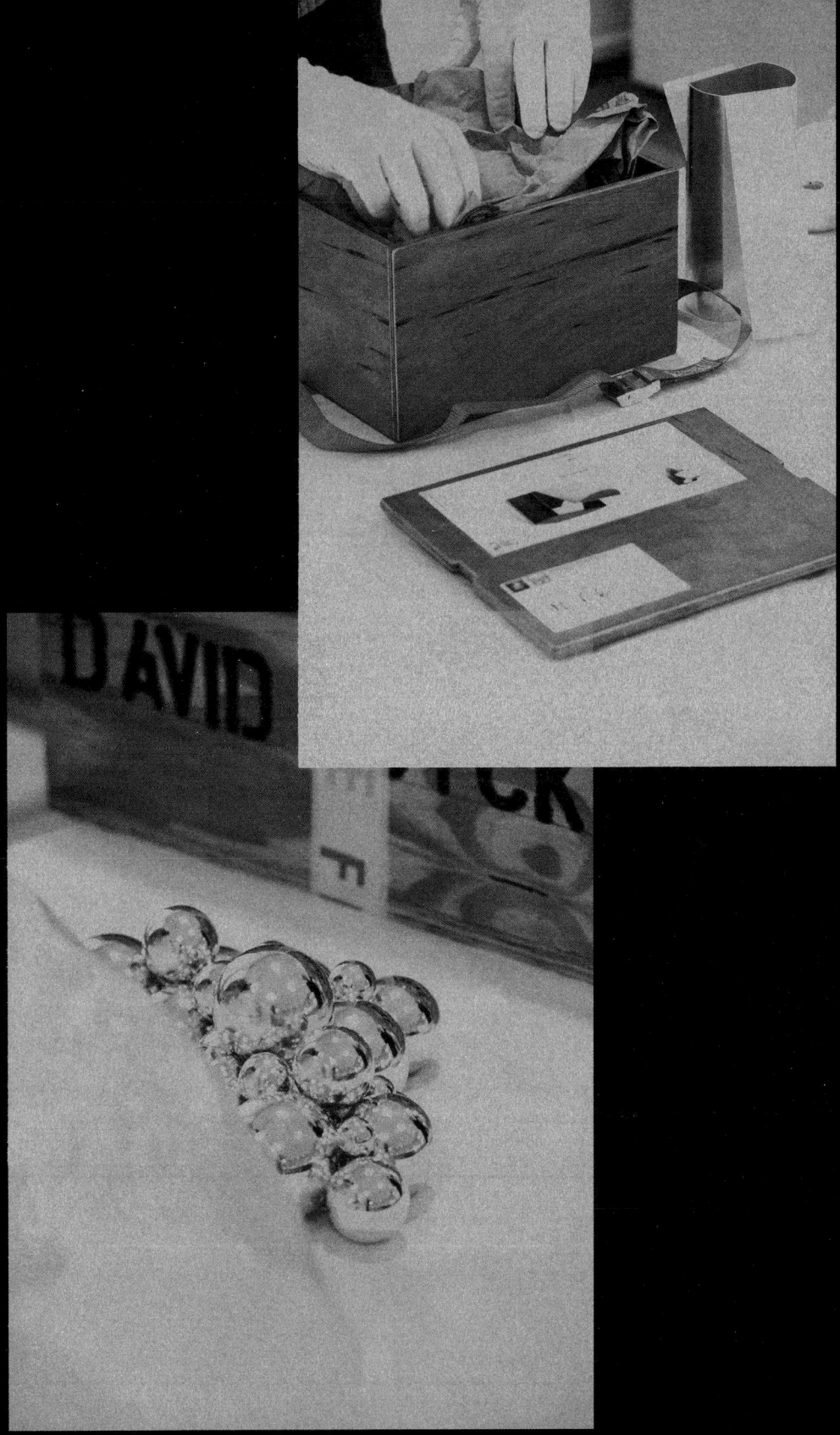

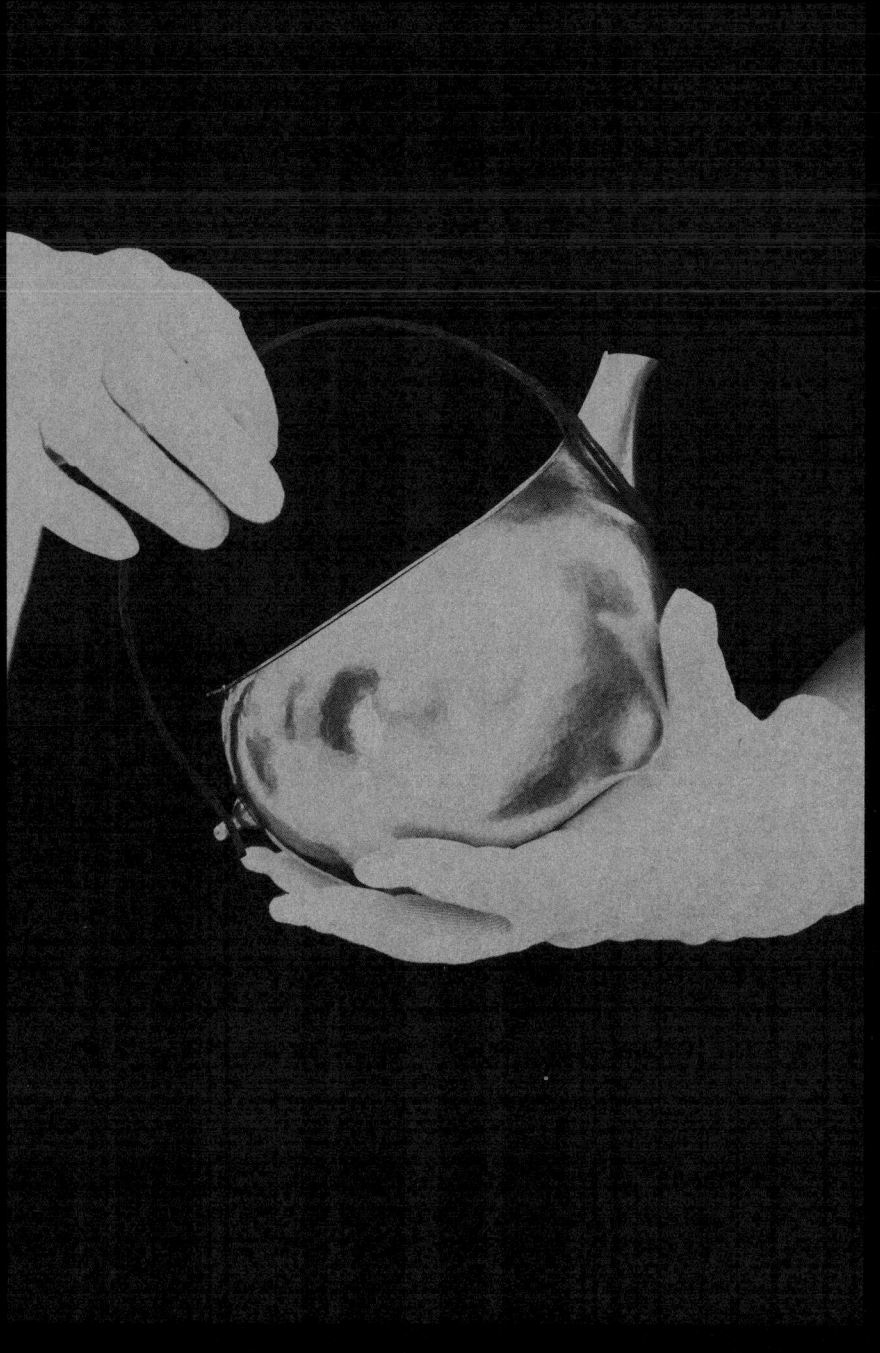

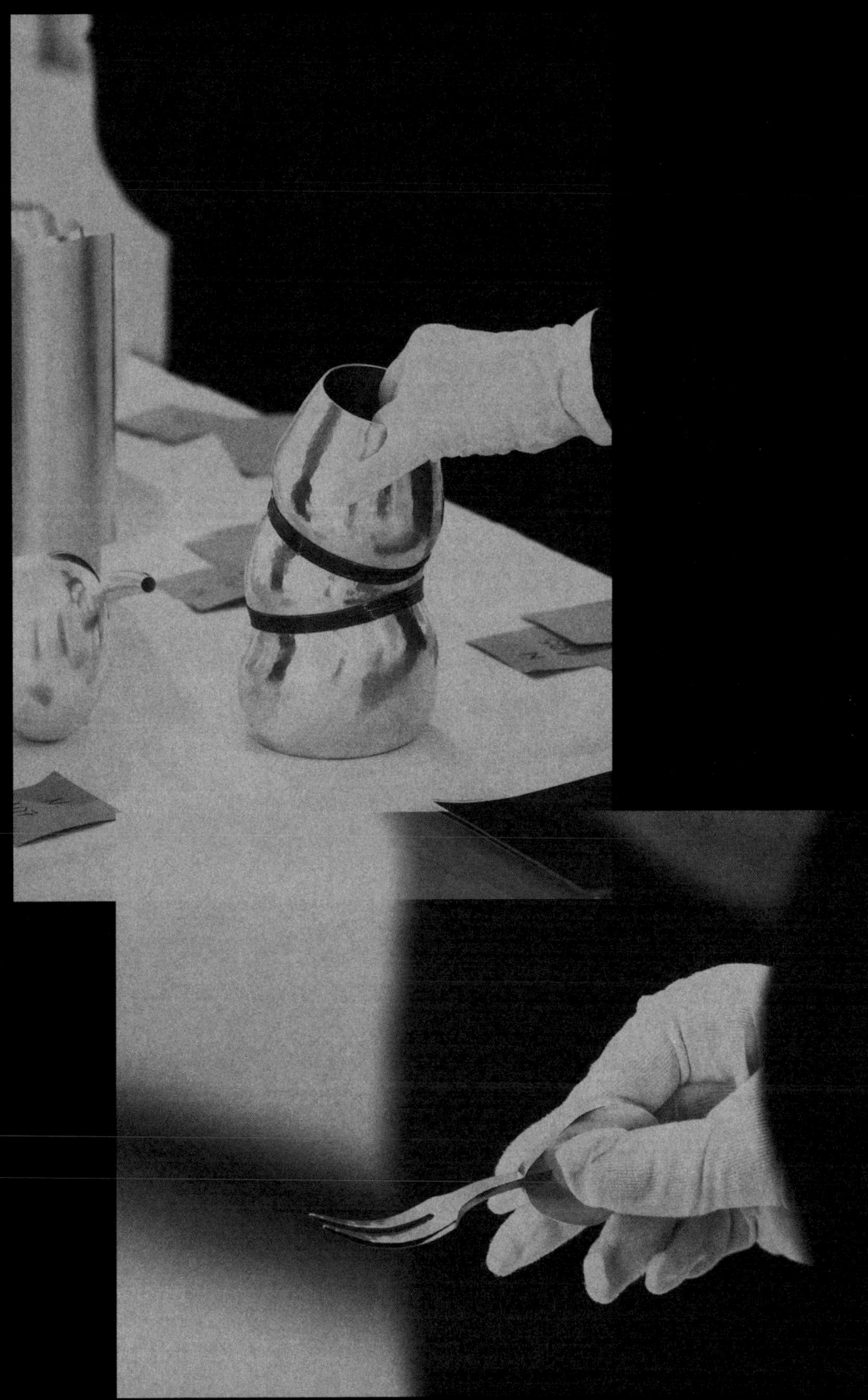

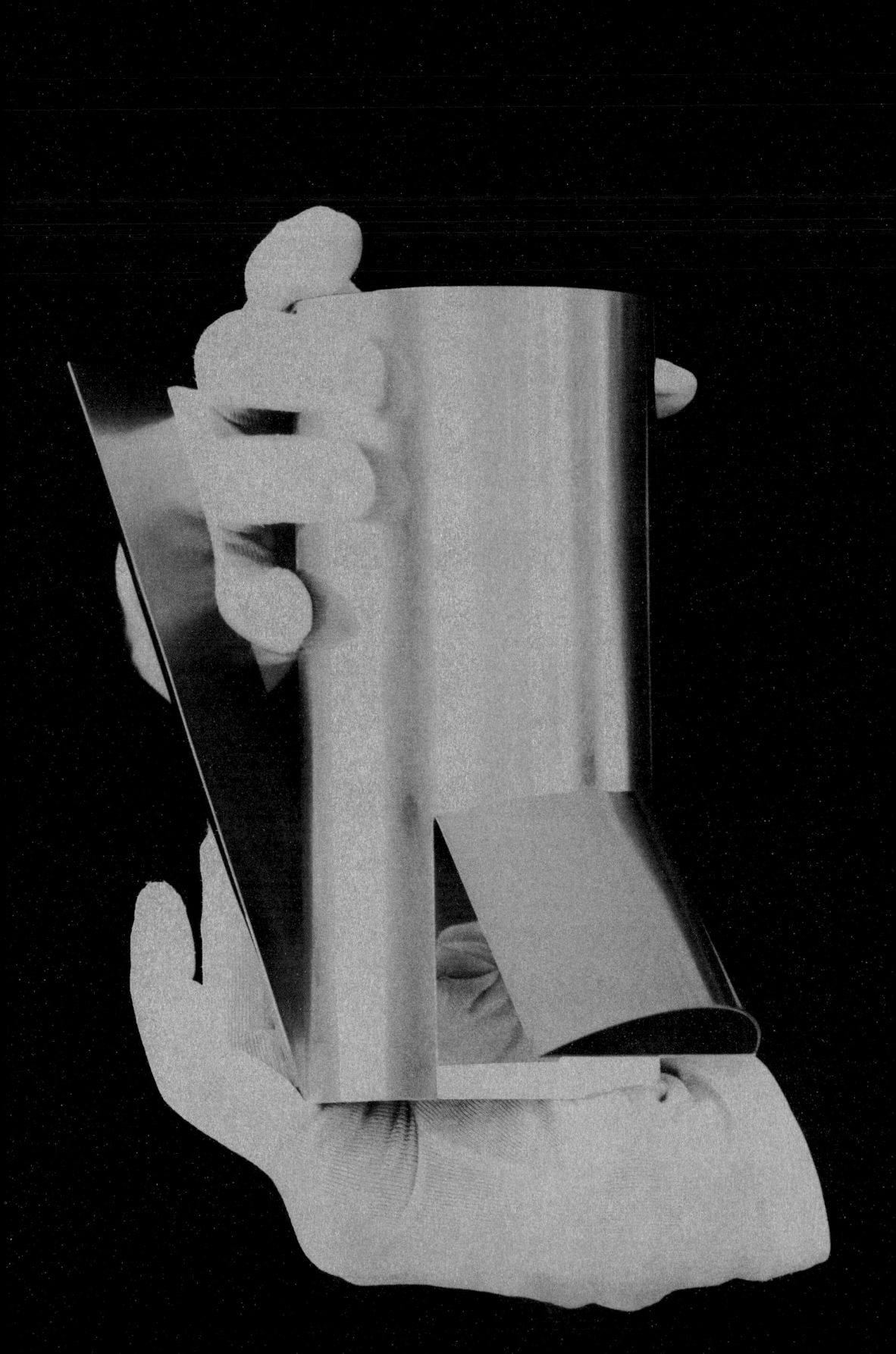

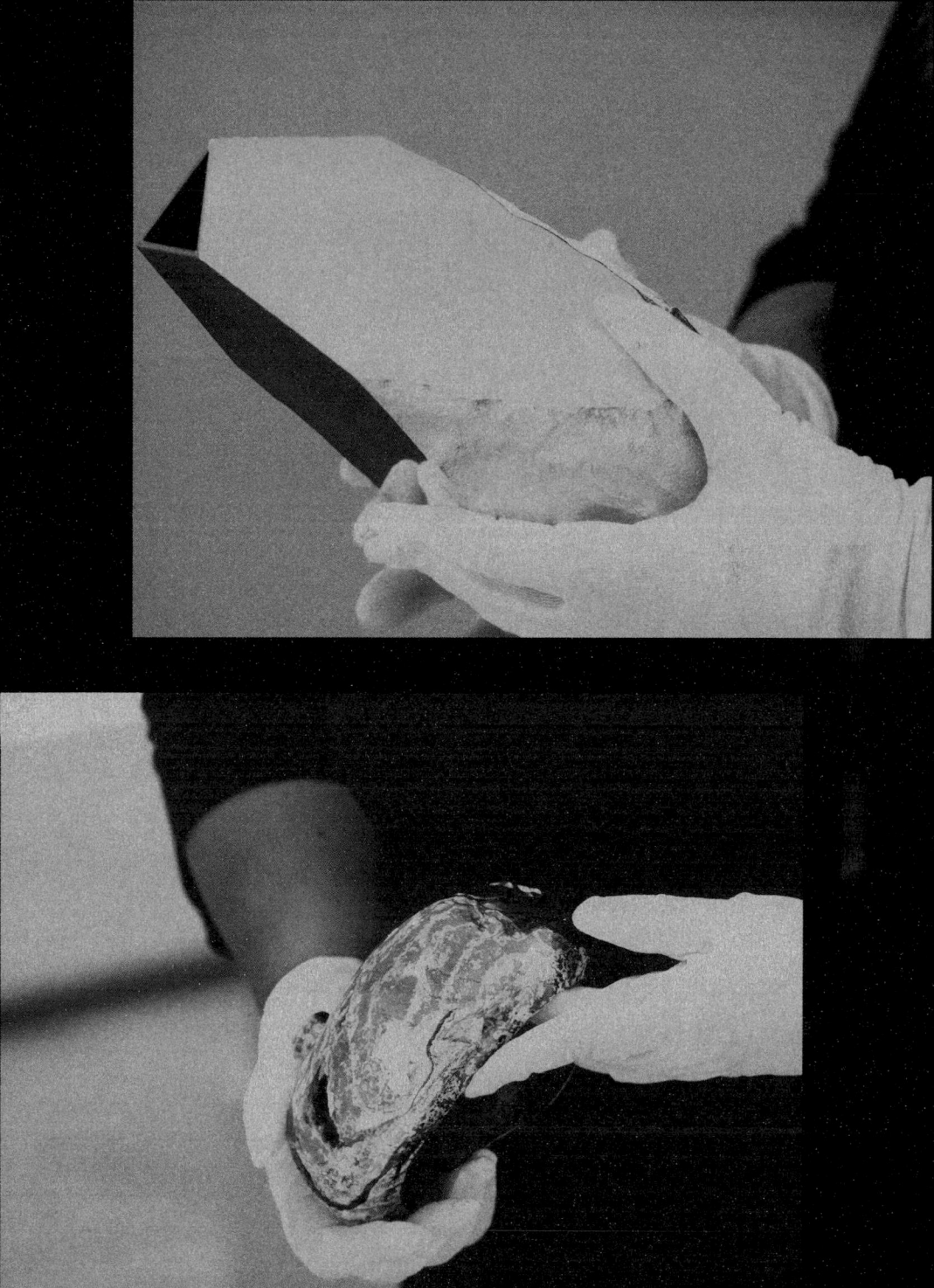

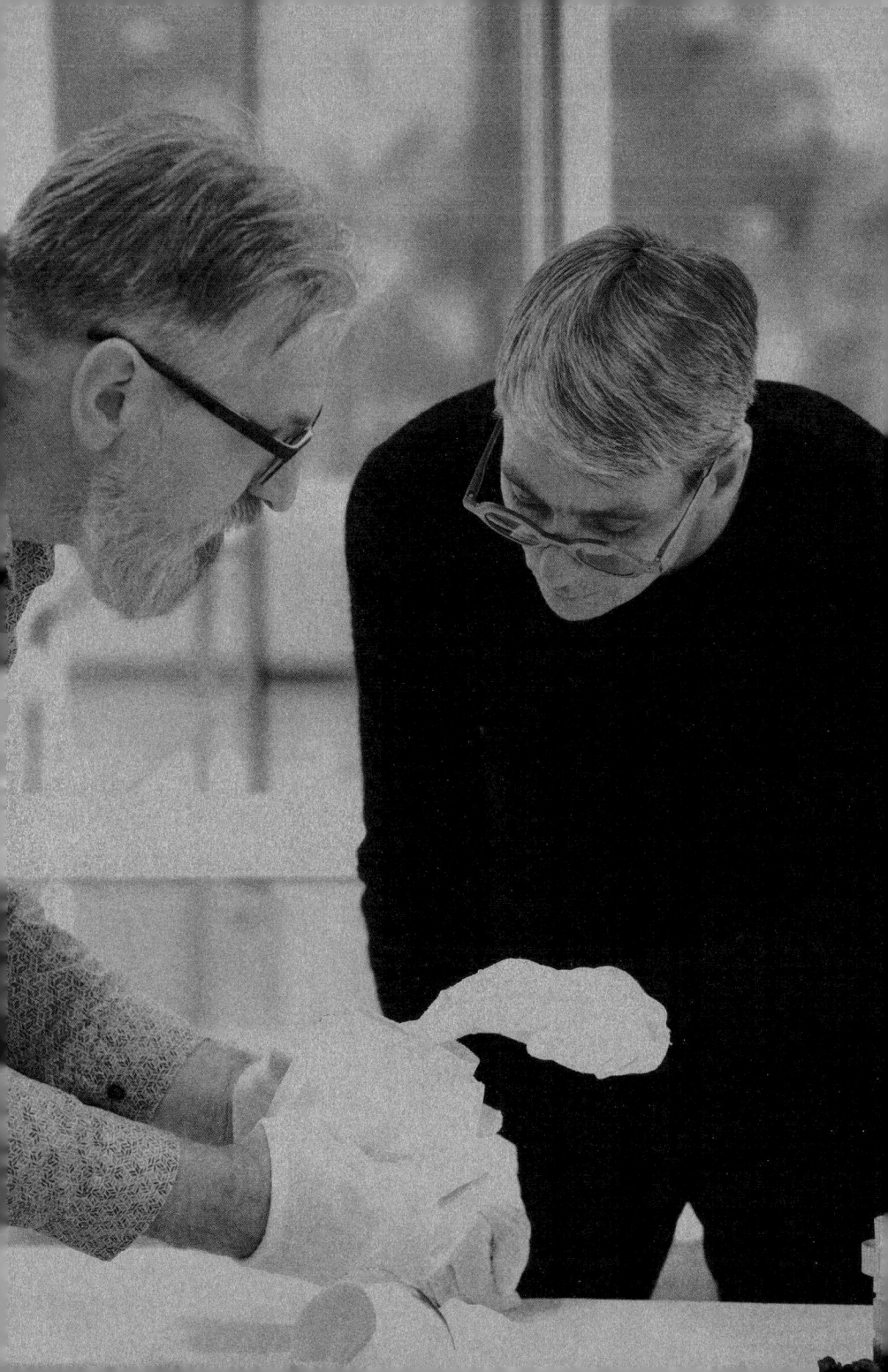

Beate Leonards

Beate Leonards (*1967) ist freischaffende Silberschmiedin und betreibt seit 1999 eine eigene Werkstatt in Lübeck. Zuvor arbeitete sie bei Georg Jensen und Allan Scharff in Kopenhagen, 2004 war sie Gastdozentin in der Gold- und Silberschmiedeklasse an der School of Art in Canberra. Nach der Ausbildung zur Silberschmiedin an der Staatlichen Zeichenakademie Hanau schloss sie 1999 ein Studium an der Akademie der Bildenden Künste in Nürnberg in der Klasse für Gold- und Silberschmieden ab.

Beate Leonards (*1967) is a freelance silversmith and has been running her own workshop in Lübeck since 1999. She previously worked for Georg Jensen and Allan Scharff in Copenhagen and in 2004 she was a guest lecturer in the gold and silversmithing class at the School of Art in Canberra. After training as a silversmith at the Staatliche Zeichenakademie Hanau, she completed her studies at the Akademie der Bildenden Künste in Nuremberg in 1999 in the class for gold and silversmithing.

Wim Nys

Wim Nys (*1969) ist seit 2016 Senior Curator und Sammlungsleiter am DIVA, Museum voor Diamant, Juwelen en Zilver in Antwerpen. Zuvor arbeitete er am Zilvermuseum Sterckshof und publizierte zu zahlreichen Themen der Gold- und Silberschmiedekunst. Er studierte Kunstgeschichte in Gent und promovierte 2015 über die Goldschmiede des Waaslandes zwischen 1688 und 1869.

Wim Nys (*1969) has been Senior Curator and Head of Collections at DIVA, Museum voor Diamant, Juwelen en Zilver in Antwerp since 2016. He previously worked at the Zilvermuseum Sterckshof and published on numerous topics relating to gold and silversmithing. He studied art history in Ghent and completed his doctorate in 2015 on the goldsmiths of Waasland between 1688 and 1869.

Karen Pontoppidan

Karen Pontoppidan (*1968) ist seit 2015 Professorin für Goldschmiedekunst an die Akademie der Bildenden Künste München, der sie seit 2022 auch als Präsidentin vorsteht. In ihrer Tätigkeit als Lehrende war sie unter anderem von 2006 bis 2015 Professorin für Schmuck und Gerät am Ädellab, Konstfack University College of Arts, Crafts and Design in Stockholm. Sie ist ausgebildet als Formgeberin für Schmuck und Gerät und hat 1998 das Studium in der Klasse von Otto Künzli an der Akademie der Bildenden Künste München mit Diplom abgeschlossen.

Karen Pontoppidan (*1968) has been Professor of Goldsmiths' Art at the Akademie der Bildenden Künste München since 2015, which she has also headed as President since 2022. Her teaching activities include being Professor of Jewellery and Corpus at Ädellab, Konstfack University College of Arts, Crafts and Design in Stockholm from 2006 to 2015. She is trained as a designer of jewelry and hollow- and flatware and graduated in 1998 from the class of Otto Künzli at the Akademie der Bildenden Künste München.

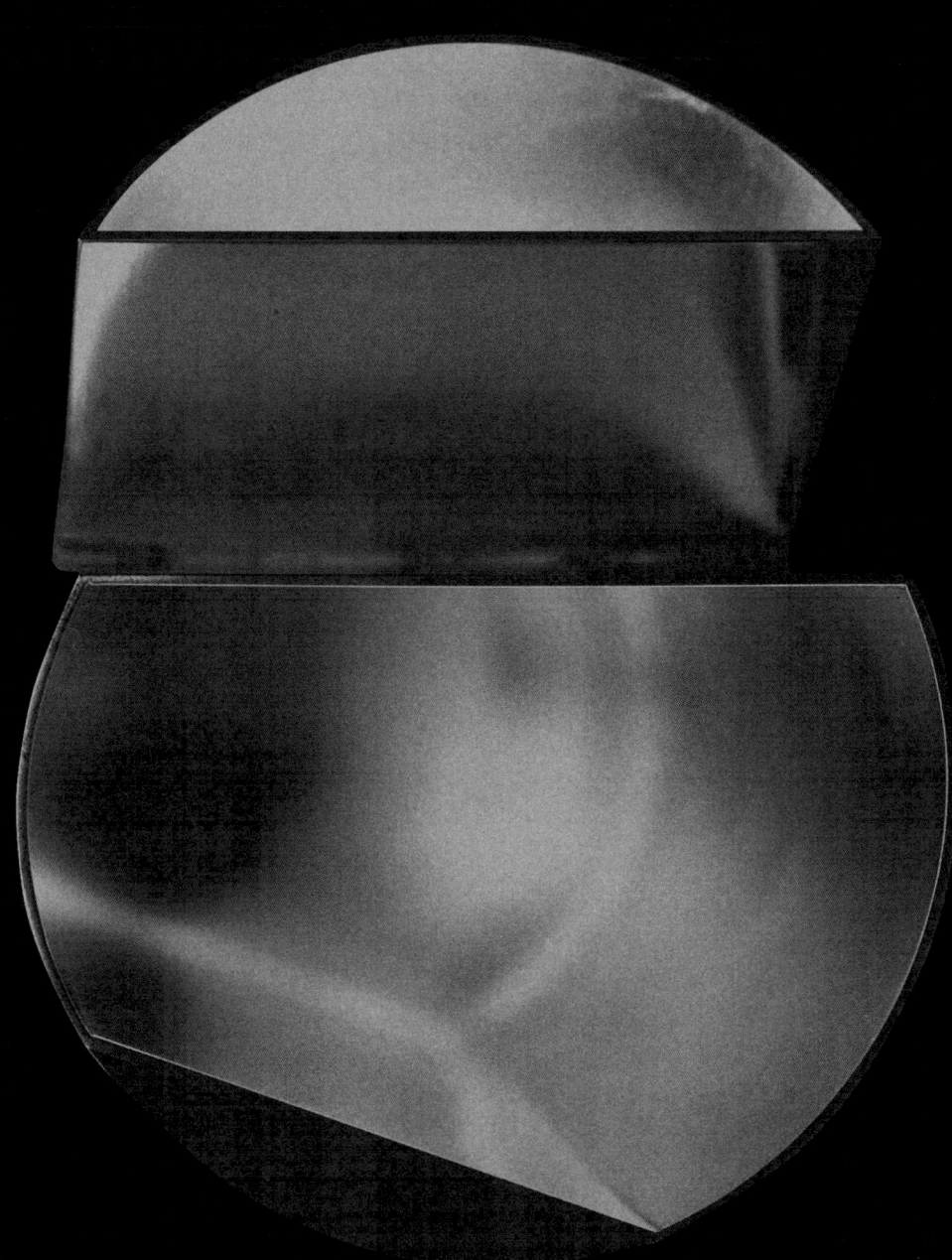

Vorwort 22
Preface 23

Hartwig Rohde

Über was wir sprechen, wenn wir Silber sagen 24

What We Talk About When We Talk About Silver 28

Malte Guttek

Jury 19

Auszeichungen
Awards

Hauptwettbewerb
Main Contest 34

Nachwuchs-
förderwettbewerb
Youth Promotion
Contest 43

Einreichungen
Submissions

Ausgewählte
Arbeiten
Selected Works 59

Werkverzeichnis
List of Works 178

Biografien
Biographies 182

Vorwort

Seit 1965 leistet die Gesellschaft für Goldschmiedekunst e.V. mit der Silbertriennale International einen wichtigen Beitrag zur Förderung des Silberschmiedens weltweit. Seit 1968 ist sie ein Kooperationsprojekt mit der Stadt Hanau, sodass mit dem Deutschen Goldschmiedehaus Hanau schon früh ein musealer Ort zur angemessenen Präsentation des Wettbewerbs zur Verfügung stand. Einen wichtigen inhaltlichen Impuls erfuhr die Silbertriennale 1992 mit der Öffnung zu einem internationalen Wettbewerb, der sich sowohl an renommierte Kunstschaffende als auch den talentierten Nachwuchs richtet. Jede Silbertriennale spiegelt eindrucksvoll das aktuelle Geschehen im Silberschmiedehandwerk wider. Dabei zeigen sich Tendenzen, wie etwa die Stärke der Silberschmiedearbeiten aus asiatischen Ländern wie Taiwan oder Südkorea, die über hervorragende Ausbildungsstätten und Universitäten verfügen. Mit der Vergabe von fünf Nachwuchspreisen verdeutlicht sich die Relevanz des Wettbewerbs für junge Gestaltende, deren Förderung eines der Hauptanliegen der Gesellschaft für Goldschmiedekunst e.V. ist.

Der Jury aus Beate Leonards, Wim Nys und Karen Pontoppidan danken wir herzlich für ihre großartige Arbeit bei der Auswahl aus 195 eingereichten Objekten und der darauffolgenden Jurierung der prämierten Wettbewerbsarbeiten.

Wir danken ebenso denen herzlich, die die Vergabe der Preise ermöglichen: für die Hauptpreise dem Nachlass Ebbe Weiss-Weingart (5.000 und 3.000 Euro) und der Firma Robbe & Berking (4.000 Euro). Für die Stiftung der Preise im Nachwuchswettbewerb danken wir dem Lions Club Hanau (3.500, 2.500 und 1.000 Euro) sowie Frau Rank (500 Euro) und wieder dem Nachlass Ebbe Weiss-Weingart (1 Kilo Silber). Ebenso danken wir den genannten wie ungenannten Förderern, die die Katalogerstellung großzügig unterstützt haben, darunter die Mannheimer Versicherung. Für die Gestaltung des Katalogs gilt unser besonderer Dank Ina Bauer Studio aus Stuttgart.

Hartwig Rohde
Präsident der Gesellschaft für Goldschmiedekunst e.V.

Preface

Since 1965, the Gesellschaft für Goldschmiedekunst e.V. has played a key role in promoting silversmithing worldwide through the Silver Triennial International. Since 1968, it has been a cooperative project with the city of Hanau, allowing the Deutsches Goldschmiedehaus Hanau to serve as an appropriate museum venue for presenting the competition from early on. The Silver Triennial took on new significance in 1992 when it expanded into an international competition open to both renowned artists and emerging talents. Each Silver Triennial impressively reflects current developments in the silversmithing craft. Notable trends have emerged, such as the growing prominence of silversmithing in Asian countries like Taiwan and South Korea, which boast outstanding training programs and universities. The awarding of five prizes for the youth competition underscores the competition's relevance for young designers whose support remains one of the core missions of the Gesellschaft für Goldschmiedekunst e.V.

We extend our sincere thanks to the jury members —Beate Leonards, Wim Nys, and Karen Pontoppidan—for their excellent work in selecting from 195 submitted objects and their subsequent jurying of the award-winning competition entries.

We are deeply grateful to those who made the prizes possible. The main awards were generously endowed by the Estate of Ebbe Weiss-Weingart (5,000 and 3,000 Euros) and Robbe & Berking (4,000 Euros). The young talent competition prizes were provided by the Lions Club Hanau (3,500, 2,500, and 1,000 Euros), Ms. Rank (500 Euros), and once more the Estate of Ebbe Weiss-Weingart (1 kilogram of silver). We also thank both named and unnamed supporters who generously contributed to the catalog's production, including Mannheimer Versicherung. Special thanks go to Ina Bauer Studio from Stuttgart for designing this catalog.

Hartwig Rohde
President of the Gesellschaft für Goldschmiedekunst e.V.

Über was wir sprechen, wenn wir Silber sagen

Es scheint ein grundsätzliches Problem zu sein, dass es vielfach am richtigen Vokabular fehlt, um über Objekte der sogenannten angewandten Kunst zu sprechen. Vielleicht liegt es daran, dass darunter sehr viele Objekte unterschiedlichster Charakteristika subsumiert werden. Dass dadurch die Trennschärfe fehlt, um sich über ihre tatsächlichen Eigenschaften und Qualitäten angemessen bewusst zu werden. Konkret fassen lässt sich dieser Umstand an der Klage über den allgemeinen Niedergang des Silbers. Diese begründet sich oft in der langen Tradition von dessen Nutzung und den dabei gemachten Erfahrungswerten. Zurecht wird angemerkt, dass es kaum noch öffentliche oder private Aufträge gibt, um das Handwerk des Silberschmiedens auf eine ausreichende wirtschaftliche Basis zu stellen.

Auch wenn allgemein über Silber, womit Gerät wie Objekt gemeint ist, gesprochen wird, ist häufig eine spezifische Form des Silbers gemeint: das Silber bürgerlicher Haushalte, die unzähligen Tabletts, Kannen und Bestecke, die in den letzten 150 Jahren entstanden sind. Die wirtschaftlichen Entwicklungen des 19. Jahrhundert schufen die Grundlage dafür, dass Silber in großer Zahl Eingang in Haushalte finden konnte und damit ein eigenes Kapitel europäischer Kulturprägung schrieb. Diese Objekte fallen in die Stilphase des Historismus, der sich durch das Aufgreifen von Stilelementen vergangener Jahrhunderte auszeichnet. Wird dessen Ende allgemein für Deutschland mit dem Ende der Monarchie 1918 gleichgesetzt, so fällt auf, dass diese kunsthistorische Phase für das Silber deutlich länger dauert und bis heute nicht abgeschlossen ist. Die Fokussierung auf diese Art der Silbergestaltung in einer breiten Öffentlichkeit reduziert die in der Silbertriennale gezeigten Objekte auf Kategorien wie Nützlichkeit oder Geschmack. Oder anders gesagt: Es wird nach dem Aufwand des Silberputzens und dem persönlichen Schönheitsempfinden gefragt. In diesem Blick verbinden sich gute wie schlechte Klischees über eine vermeintliche Bürgerlichkeit. Es wird dabei aber explizit auf Gebrauchssilber geschaut, dessen Rezeption für die Wahrnehmung künstlerisch hervortretender Silbergestaltung nicht geeignet ist und so keine Perspektive im Sprechen über zeitgenössisches Silber bietet.

Zu diesem verengenden Blick gesellt sich eine weitere Problematik. Die Zuschreibung von künstlerisch hervortretendem Silber in Kategorien wie angewandte Kunst, Kunstgewerbe oder Kunsthandwerk beinhaltet in sich eine Limitierung. Die Objekte werden sprachlich mit einem Makel behaftet, der sie der angemessenen Auseinandersetzung entzieht, wie es für viele andere Gattungen der Kunst selbstverständlich ist. Die aus den vorherigen Jahrhunderten überkommenen Silberobjekte wurden insbesondere mit der aufkommenden Akademisierung der Kunstgeschichte im 19. Jahrhundert der angewandten Kunst zugewiesen. Infolgedessen wurde in ihrer Charakterisierung der Gebrauchswert und Entstehungskontext als klassifizierende Kategorie bestimmend. So wird mit repräsentativen Tafelgeschirr oder prächtigen Schauobjekten in den Museen der angewandten Kunst die Entwicklung von Ornamenten erläutert, technische Innovation dargestellt oder anekdotisch von ihrer Provenienz berichtet. Dieser Umstand mag auch in der Entstehungsgeschichte dieser Museen begründet sein, die ursprünglich als Vorbildsammlungen für das Handwerk und die Industrie initiiert wurden. Mit diesem Verzwecken im Sinne einer beschränkenden musealen Erzählung oder erzieherischen Wirkung können sie aber selten aus sich heraus ihren künstlerischen Wert sprechen lassen, ihre Qualität vor den Betrachtenden entfalten.

Was den Objekten vielfach fehlt, ist ein unvoreingenommener Blick auf sie. Es mangelt an Fragen nach Themen, die über ihre materielle Erscheinung hinausgehen. In den Museen für angewandte Kunst ist das künstlerisch hervortretende Silber vergangener Jahrhunderte seinem ursprünglichen Funktionszusammenhang entzogen. Schauen wir auf andere Museen, etwa Schlösser mit erhaltenen Ausstattungen, dann befindet sich das Silber noch in seinem ursprünglichen Kontext. Hier wird es jedoch noch deutlicher: Mit der Musealisierung sind die Objekte den komplexen Ebenen ihrer Funktion beraubt. Zwar lässt sich im Ausstellungsraum noch erahnen, welche Wirkung eine prächtig eingedeckte Tafel hatte. Es wird aber nicht mehr wahrgenommen, dass die dafür genutzten Objekte nicht einfach dekoratives Gerät zur reinen Essensaufnahme waren. Vielmehr hatten diese Objekte einen performativen Charakter, der in ihrer Nutzung, ihrer Betrachtung und dem Sprechen über sie eine entscheidende Rolle in der Gesellschaft ihrer Entstehungszeit spielten.

Den Fokus auf solche soziologischen und kulturellen Aspekte zu wenden, kann ein Beginn sein, die Qualität von Silberschmiedearbeiten auf Augenhöhe zu anderen Künsten zu ergründen. Wenn dies für das bereits museale Silber in einer größeren Breite gelingt, können daraus erhebliche Impulse für die Gegenwart erwachsen. Mit einem anderen Blick auf Silber können die Sinne geschärft werden. Hervorragend gestaltetes Gerät und neugierig machende Objekte stehen in dieser Silbertriennale überraschend nebeneinander, sie machen die Vielfalt der Silberanwendung aus. An den ausgewählten Arbeiten wird ein Ringen in der Form, der Oberflächengestaltung und der Themen von großer Vielfalt ersichtlich. Dieses künstlerisch hervortretende Silber ist in der Lage, zwischen den anderen Künsten zu bestehen. Es muss aber nicht nur mit diesem anerkennenden Blick betrachtet werden, es muss auch so darüber gesprochen werden.

Malte Guttek
Geschäftsführer Gesellschaft für Goldschmiedekunst e.V.
Leiter Deutsches Goldschmiedehaus Hanau

What We Talk About When We Talk About Silver

In talking about objects of so-called applied art, we face a fundamental challenge: the lack of appropriate vocabulary to discuss these objects meaningfully. This limitation might stem from the category's vast scope, encompassing objects with widely varying characteristics. The resulting imprecision makes it difficult to articulate their true properties and qualities. This challenge becomes particularly evident in lamentations about silver's perceived decline. These are often grounded in the experience of its long-standing tradition. In contrast, people correctly note today's scarcity of public and private commissions necessary to sustain silversmithing as a viable craft.

Discussions of silver, meaning utensils as well as objects, often focus narrowly on a specific type of silver: the domestic silver of bourgeois households—the trays, pitchers, and cutlery that proliferated over the past 150 years. The economic growth of the 19th century enabled silver's widespread entry into private homes, marking a distinctive period in European cultural development. These objects emerged during the era of Historicism, characterized by its revival of historical styles. While in Germany, the end of this phase is commonly equated with the fall of the monarchy in 1918, its influence on silver design has persisted remarkably longer, extending into the present day. The focus on traditional domestic silver among the general public tends to reduce the works featured in the Silver Triennial to considerations of utility or taste. Questions revolve around practical concerns like the effort required to polish silver or personal aesthetic preferences, reinforcing good and bad clichés about supposed bourgeois values. This perspective is ill-suited to the appreciation of artistic silver design and offers no meaningful framework for discussing contemporary silver.

This narrow view is compounded by another problem: placing artistic silver into categories such as applied art, decorative arts, or artisan crafts inherently restricts its perception. These labels hinder the objects' ability to receive the serious critical attention routinely granted to other art forms. When academic art history emerged in the 19th century, silver objects handed down from bygone centuries were assigned to the category of applied arts. This led to an emphasis on utility value and production context as primary criteria for classification. Consequently, in applied arts museums, representative tableware and resplendent exhibition objects serve to illustrate ornamental development, showcase technical innovation, or provide anecdotal accounts of their provenance. This approach may reflect these institutions' origins as reference collections for craftspeople and industry. However, framing these objects within a restrictive museum narrative or educational purpose rarely allows them to express their inherent artistic value or fully reveal their qualities to viewers.

What these objects lack is unprejudiced examination. Inquiries into themes that reach beyond their material properties are scarce. In applied arts museums, artistic silver of centuries past is removed from its original functional contexts. Even in preserved palace settings, where silver remains in its historical environment, the process of musealization deprives the objects of their complex functional dimensions. While viewers might sense the impressive effect of an elaborately set table, they often miss that these objects were more than decorative tableware for dining. These pieces had a performative quality, shaping the way they were used, displayed, and spoken about and playing a crucial role in the societies in which they originated.

Shifting our focus towards these sociological and cultural dimensions offers a pathway to understanding silversmithing as equal to other forms of art. Successfully broadening this perspective on musealized silver could inspire significant momentum for the present. A renewed outlook on silver sharpens our perception. In this Silver Triennial, exquisitely designed functional objects stand alongside thought-provoking artistic objects, demonstrating silver's diverse applications. The selected works reveal a sophisticated engagement with form, surface, and a striking diversity of themes. These artistically significant silver pieces can hold their own among other art forms. They should not only be regarded with an appreciative eye but also spoken about with equal recognition.

Malte Guttek
General Manager of the Gesellschaft für Goldschmiedekunst e.V.
Director of the Deutsches Goldschmiedehaus Hanau

Hauptwettbewerb
Main Contest

Yeunhee Ryu
Yong-il Jeon
Jieun Park

Nachwuchsförderwettbewerb
Youth Promotion Contest

Yegyu Shin
Siqiu Zhang
Jae Hui Jeong
Carl Kankowsky
Rebecca Bierbrodt

Yeunhee Ryu

Kanne
Jug

Goryeo 2

Ebbe Weiss-Weingart
Preis / Prize

Jury Statement
Die Verweigerung des Perfekten in der Gestaltung der Kanne führt zu einer ganz eigenen, intuitiven Ästhetik von hoher Überzeugungskraft. Mit Könnerschaft ist ein erzählerisches Objekt entstanden, das den Eindruck eines alten, gebrauchten Gegenstandes erzeugt. Diese imaginierte Zeitlichkeit hat unter der Vielzahl von hervorragenden Objekten die Jury emotional am stärksten berührt.

> The refusal of perfection in the design of the jug leads to a very unique, intuitive aesthetic of great persuasiveness. A narrative object has been skilfully created that gives the impression of an old, used jug. This imagined temporality touched the jury most emotionally among the many outstanding objects.

Yeunhee Ryu

Jury Statement
Die hervorragende Interpretation der klassischen Teekanne überzeugt durch Reduktion, das sensible Spiel zwischen den Grautönen der Materialien ist berührend. Feinfühlig wurde für jedes Detail eine gelungene Lösung gefunden, die sich im raffinierten Aufbau zeigt. So stellt die Handhabe des Deckels eine ungewohnte, aber funktionale Lösung dar.

The outstanding interpretation of the classic teapot is convincing through its reduction, the sensitive interplay between the gray tones of the materials is touching. A successful solution has been sensitively found for every detail, which is reflected in the refined design. The lid handle, for example, is an unusual but functional solution.

Yong-il Jeon

Yong-il Jeon

Teekanne
Teapot

*Tea pot with
a nickel handle*

39

**Robbe & Berking
Preis / Prize**

Jieun Park

Gefäß
Vessel

The flexible vessel
2372

41

Ebbe Weiss-Weingart
Silberpreis / Silver Price

Jury Statement
Der ungewöhnliche Aufbau des dreibeinigen Behältnisses löst einen Moment der Überraschung aus, wenn es in die Hand genommen wird: Es ist hart und weich zugleich. Ohne seine Grundform zu verändern, beeinflusst die Schwerkraft seine Form. Im Detail überzeugt die individuelle Ausführung der einzelnen Elemente, die zahlreiche Assoziationen hervorruft.

The unusual structure of the three-legged container triggers a moment of surprise when it is picked up: it is hard and soft at the same time. Without changing its basic shape, gravity influences its form. The design of the individual elements is impressive in detail and evokes numerous associations.

Jieun
Park

Jury Statement
Die Arbeit greift das Thema des Löffels auf und befragt diesen nach seiner tieferen Bedeutung. Dabei steht nicht die klassische Funktion der Nahrungsaufnahme im Fokus, sondern das Motiv des Weitergebens. So lässt die Reihung vielfältige Assoziationen zu. Der fragile und sensible Aufbau aus Silber und rotem Faden erzeugt ein Gefühl von Zuwendung.

The work takes up the theme of the spoon and questions its deeper meaning. The focus is not on the classic function of food intake, but on the motif of passing it on. The arrangement allows for a variety of associations. The fragile and sensitive structure of silver and red thread creates a feeling of affection.

Yegyu Shin

Yegyu
Shin•

Objekt
Object

Toy of Time I

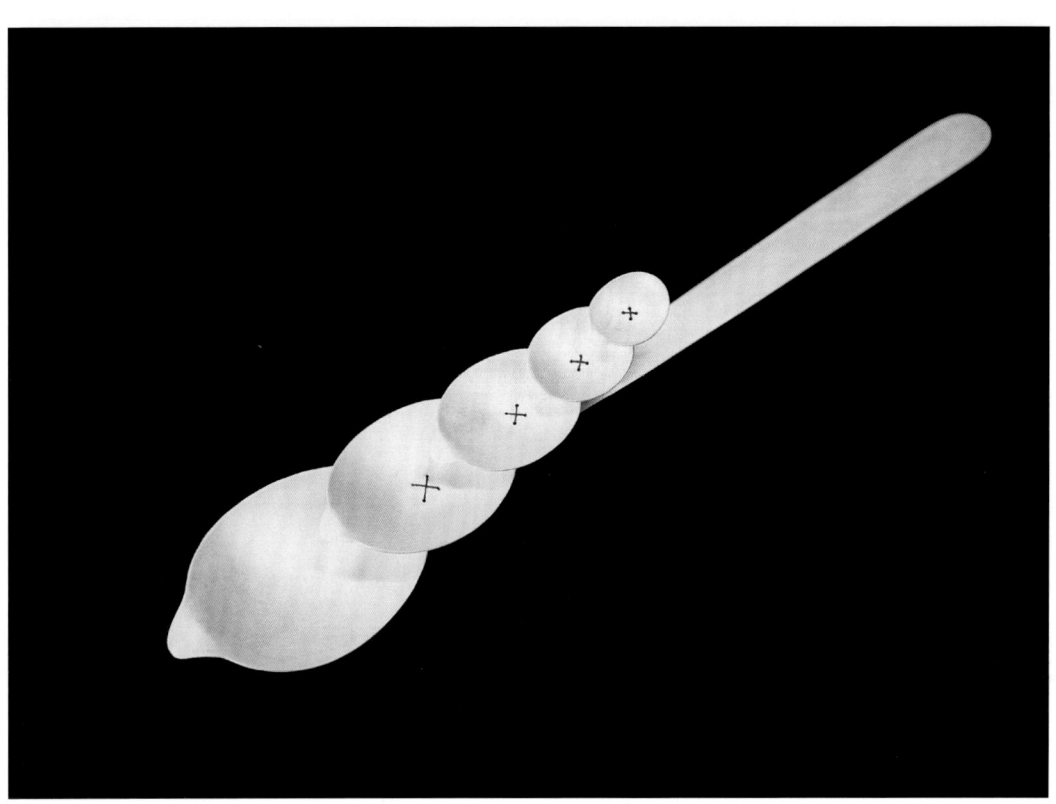

1. Lions Club Hanau
Nachwuchsförderpreis
1st Lions Club Hanau
Youth Promotion Prize

Siqiu Zhang•

Vase *shimmering* 47

2. Lions Club Hanau
Nachwuchsförderpreis
2nd Lions Club Hanau
Youth Promotion Prize

Jury Statement
Die Arbeit überzeugt mit ihrer Dekoration, die zur Form selbst wird. Die hohe Qualität der handwerklichen und gestalterischen Ausführung in Silberdraht erzeugt eine fragile Oberfläche von transluzider Wirkung. Sie erzeugt im Wechselspiel mit der klassischen Vasenform ein großes Spannungsfeld von Öffnungen und Verschlüssen.

The work impresses with its decoration, which becomes the form itself. The high quality of the craftsmanship and design in silver wire creates a fragile surface with a translucent effect. In the interplay with the classic vase shape, it creates a large field of tension between openings and closures.

Siqiu Zhang

Jury Statement
Die Schale thematisiert das ihr innewohnende
Grundthema von Innen und Außen, von Druck und
Gegendruck. Ihre komplexe und dennoch ruhige Form
lässt die Energie erahnen, die sie von innen heraus in
Form gebracht hat. Ihre technische Präzision erzeugt
den Eindruck von großer Leichtigkeit.
   The bowl thematizes the inherent basic theme of
inside and outside, of pressure and counter-pressure.
Its complex yet calm form hints at the energy that
has molded it from the inside out. Its technical
precision creates the impression of great lightness.

Jae Hui
Jeong

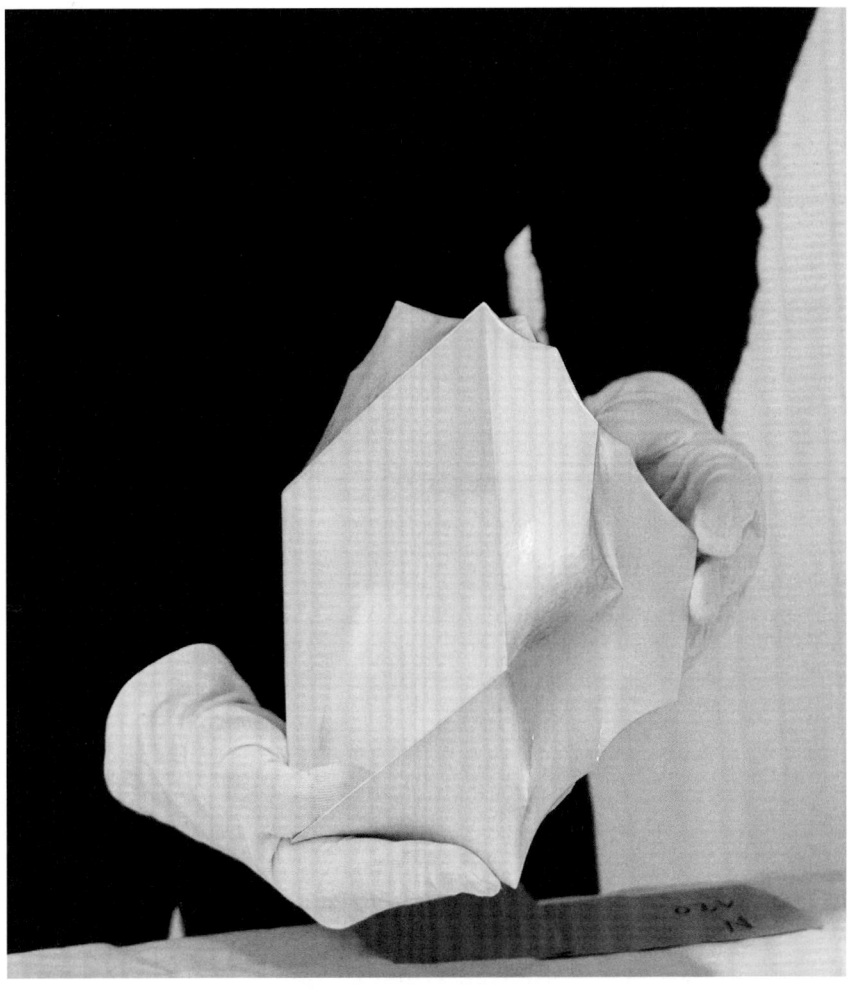

Jae Hui Jeong•

Schale
Bowl

Conceal and Reveal

3. Lions Club Hanau Nachwuchsförderpreis
3rd Lions Club Hanau Youth Promotion Prize

Carl Kankowsky•

Kanne
Jug

Ebbe Weiss-Weingart
Silberpreis / Silver Prize

Jury Statement
Die auf den ersten Blick simple Form der Kanne offenbart bei der genauen Betrachtung eine komplexe Herleitung. Aus der geometrischen Form des Zylinders sind die funktional notwendigen Bestandteile Griff und Ausguss durch gezielt gesetzte Schnitte herausgelöst. Die Kanne ist eine überzeugende Neuinterpretation eines klassischen Geräts.

At first glance, the jug's simple shape reveals a complex derivation on closer inspection. The handle and spout, which are functionally necessary components, have been removed from the geometric shape of the cylinder by means of carefully placed cuts. The jug is a convincing reinterpretation of a classic appliance.

Carl Kankowsky

Jury Statement
Die Arbeit erweckt die Vorstellung, dass ihre Form unter dem Druck des Silberdrahtes auf den Korpus entstanden ist. Sie wirkt fluid, noch nicht abgeschlossen. Dieses erzählerische Motiv lässt weitere Eingriffe noch möglich erscheinen. Im Zusammenspiel mit den Farbkontrasten verleihen sie der Arbeit ästhetische Spannung.

    The work gives the impression that its form was created under the pressure of the silver wire on the body. It appears fluid, not yet finalized. This narrative motif makes further interventions seem possible. In combination with the color contrasts, they lend the work aesthetic tension.

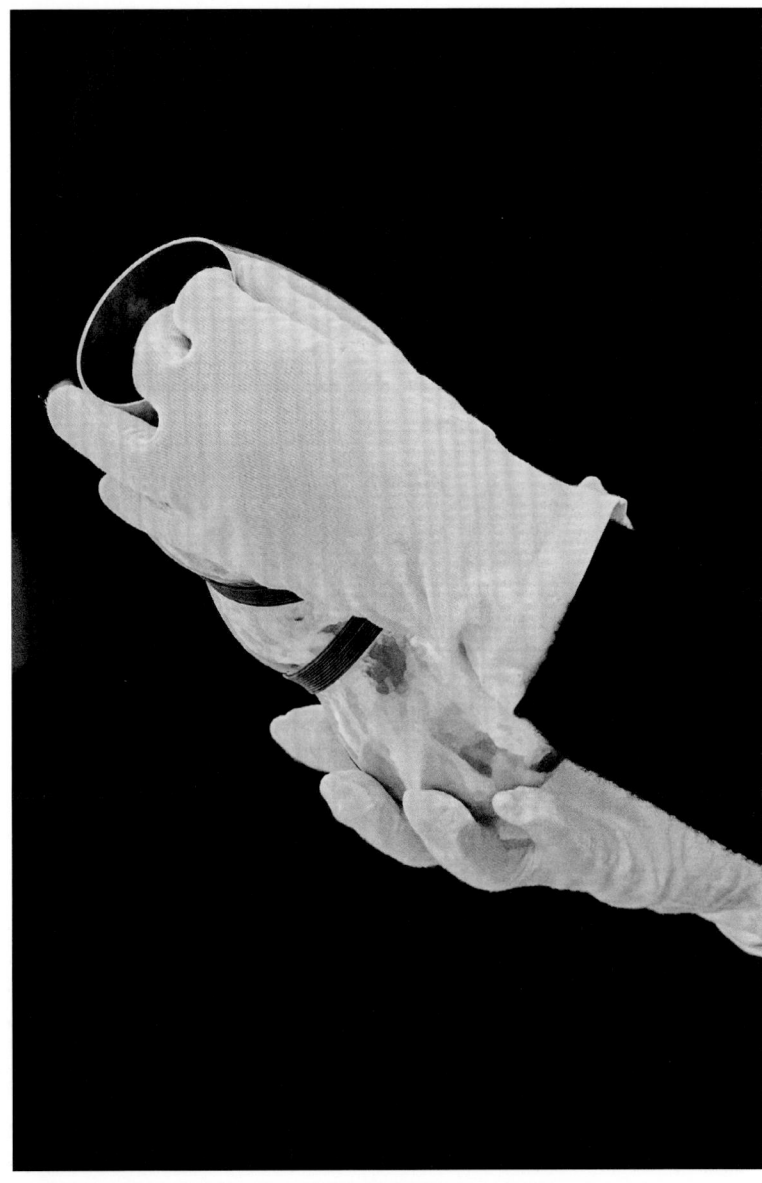

Rebecca Bierbrodt

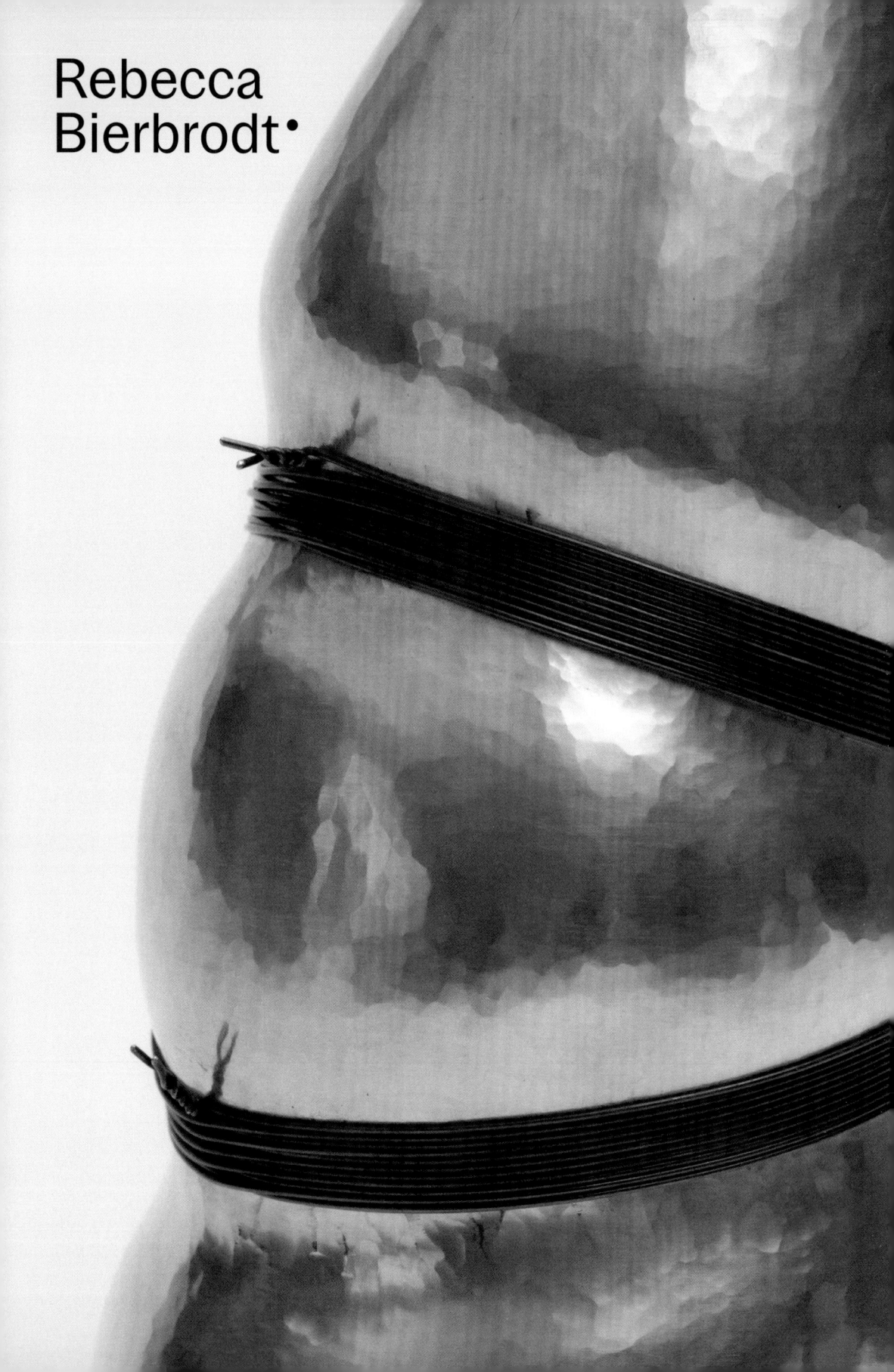

Rebecca
Bierbrodt•

Gefäß / Vessel

Angst

57

Rank'sche Preis / Prize

Farah Abdelhamid·
Eckhard Adler
Min Sick Ahn
Ana Albuquerque
Barbara Amstutz
Ralf Auerbach
Hyun Baek
Eva Bauer
Gitte Bjørn
Emil Borregaard
Tabea Helena Maki
  Brindöpke·
Ya-Ping Cheng·
Sungho Cho
Sarah Cossham
Andreas Decker
Hanyi Feng·
Gretal Ferguson
Benedikt
  Förster-Heyne
Andreas Frank
Luise Fritzsche·
Kristóf András Gelley
Kirsten Haydon
Jiahn Hong·
Marian Hosking
Iris Hummer
David Huycke
Inhwan Jeon·
Sang Hoon Kim
Catherine Large

Annette Lechler
Zhizhong Li·
Bo-Ting Lin·
Qiwei Liu·
Christine Matthias
Militsa Milenkova &
  Callum Partridge·
Alex O'Connor
Byungik Park·
Wu Peng·
Christoph Pilsel·
Christine Ramel
Yeunhee Ryu
Helena Schepens
Juliane Schölß
Gerrit Schulze
  Raestrup·
Regina Eva Sebold·
Yegyu Shin
Oliver Smith
Mariko Sumioka
Lee Sungyeoul
Mohammad Taghavi·
Christoph Weißhaar
Tong Wu·

· Nachwuchswettbewerb
  Youth Promotion Contest

Farah
Abdelhamid•

Objekt
Object

Bi-form 1

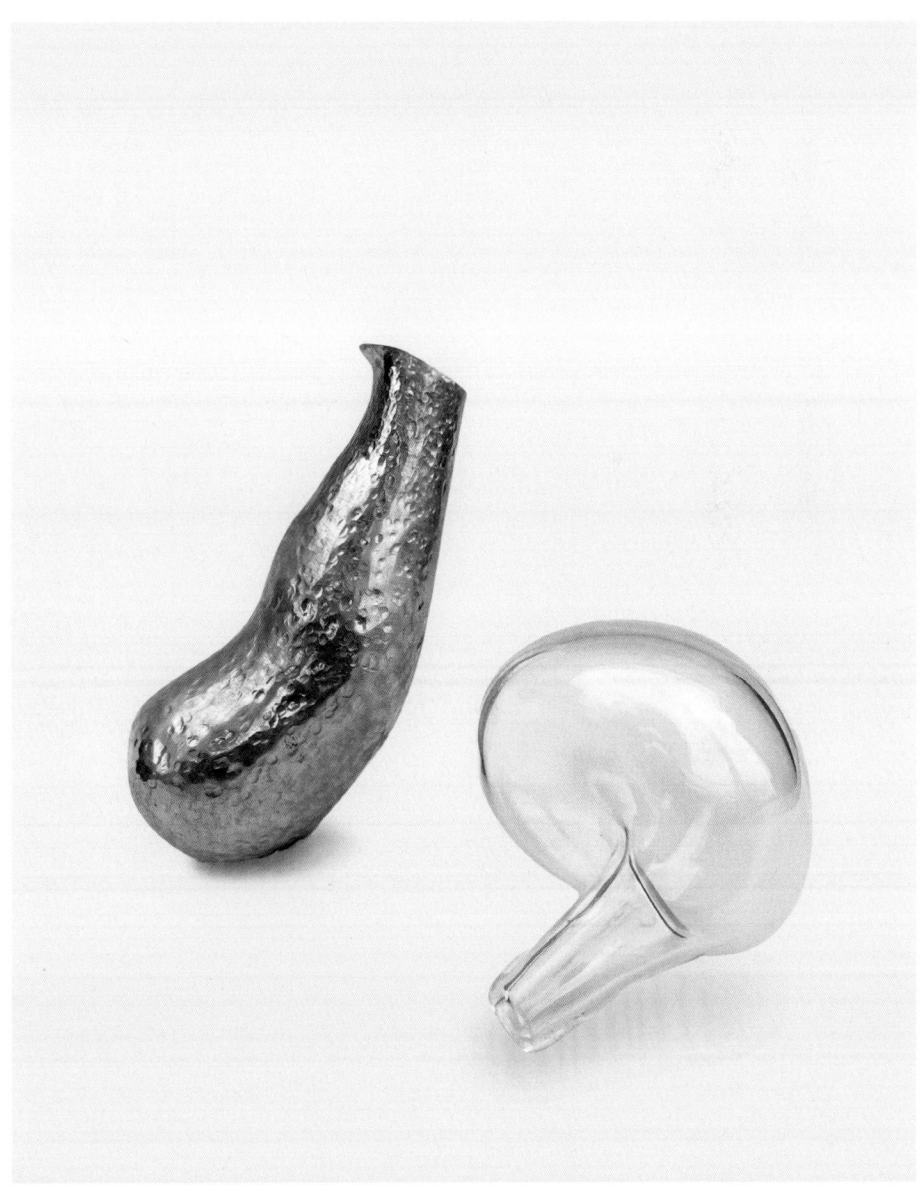

Eckhard Adler

Teekanne
Teapot

Teekanne

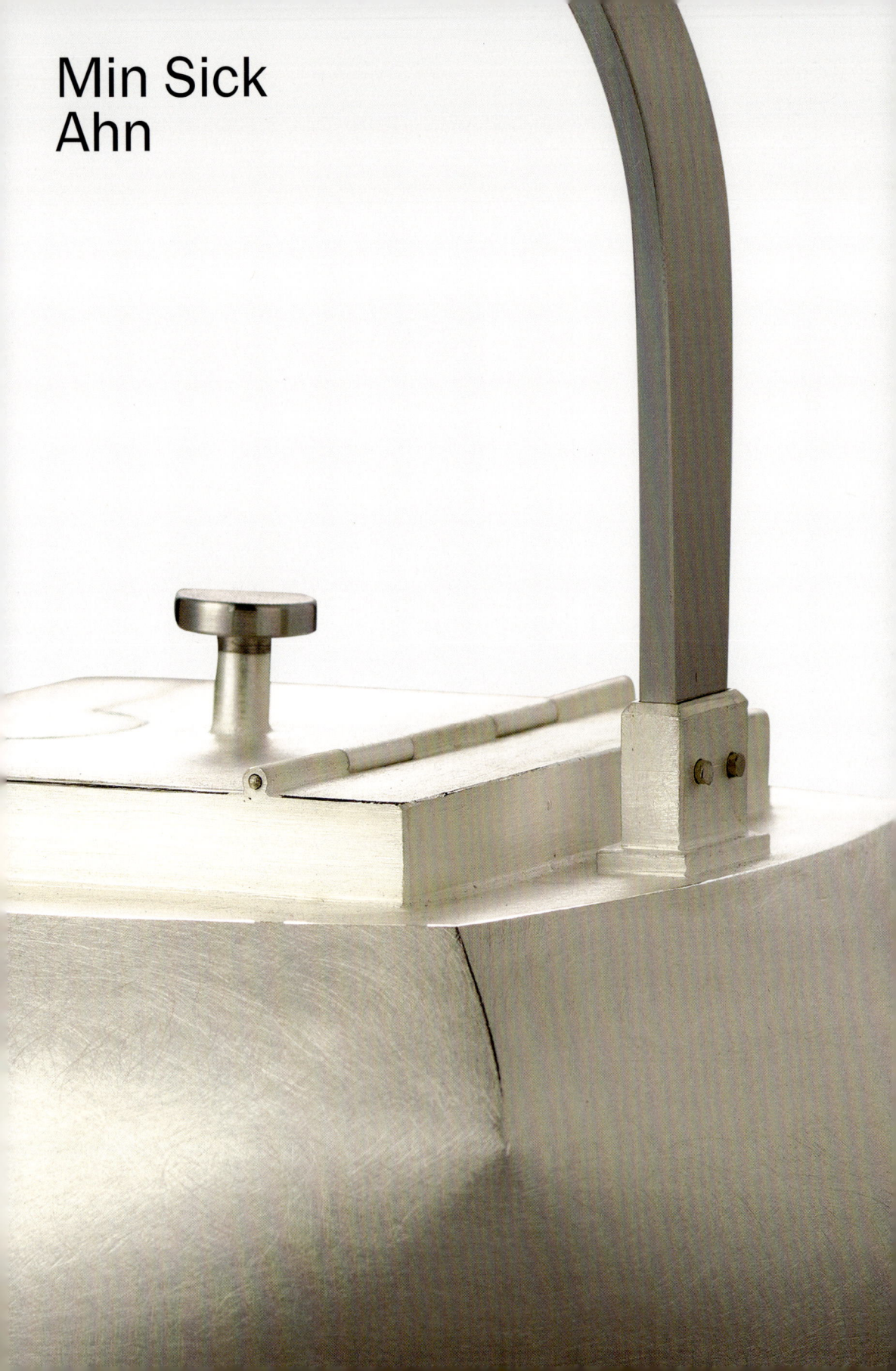

Min Sick Ahn

Kessel
Kettle

*Silver Kettle
2023*

65

Ana Albuquerque

Objekt
Object

restart

Barbara Amstutz

Karaffe
Carafe

Karaffe 2024

Ralf
Auerbach

Schale
Bowl

Schale 160

Hyun
Baek

Vase

Timespace vase

Eva Bauer

Studie *Goldi*
Study

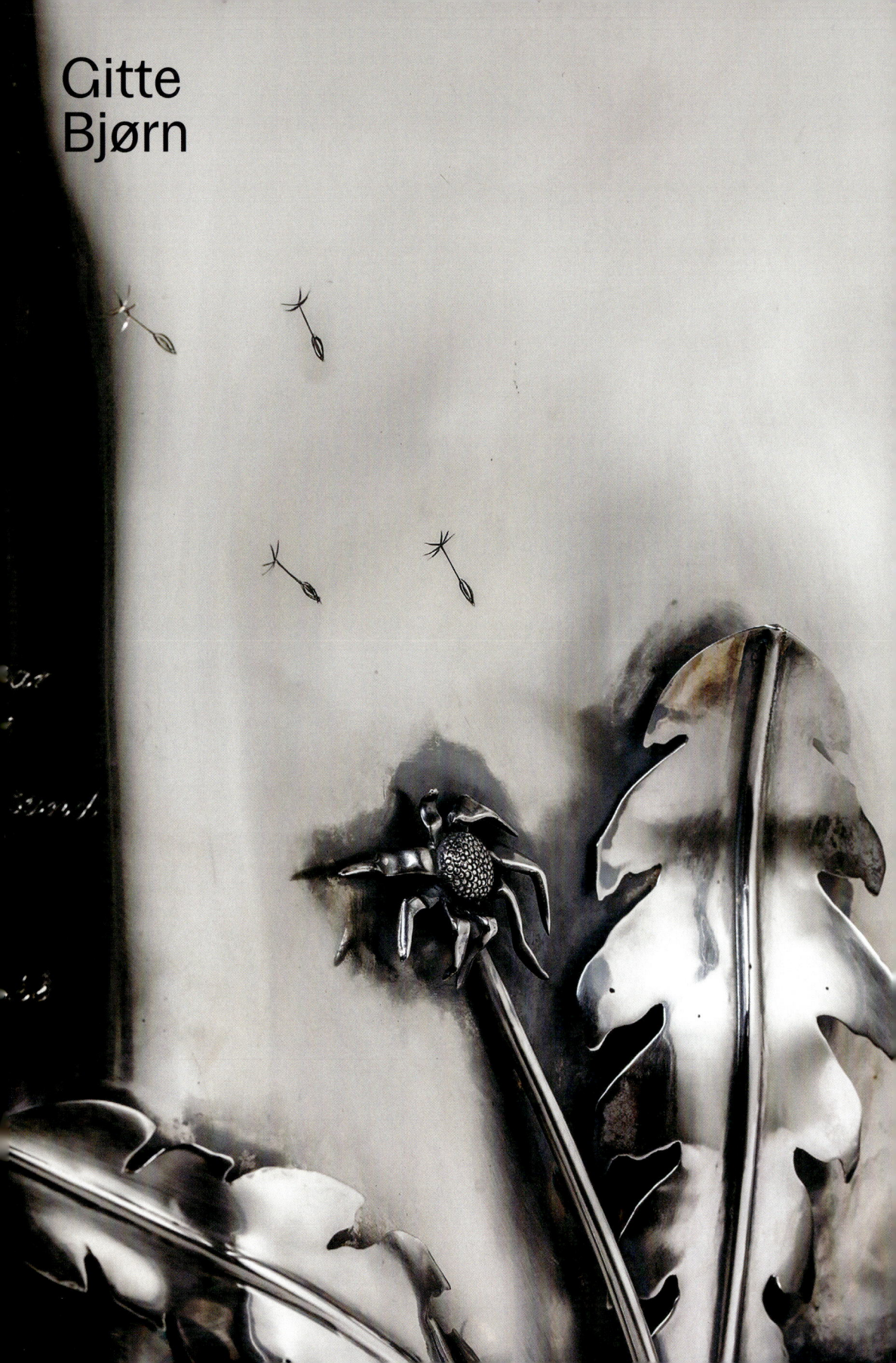

Gitte Bjørn

Urne Anywhere Else
Urn

Schale
Bowl

Giffelfad

Tabea Helena Maki
Brindöpke•

Milchkanne
Milk jug

Coffee & Games

Ya-Ping Cheng•

Vase

Ya-Ping
Cheng•

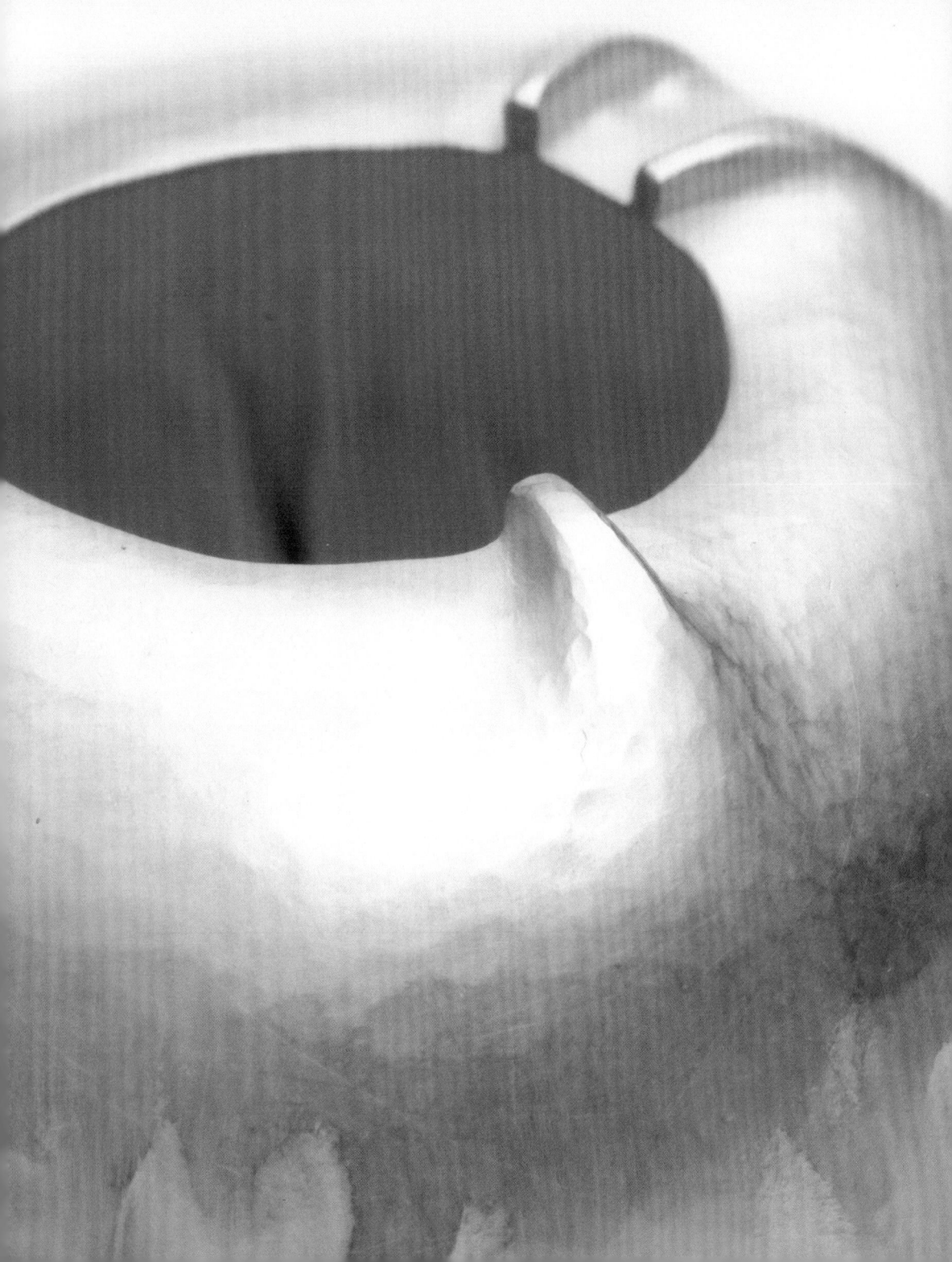

Vase

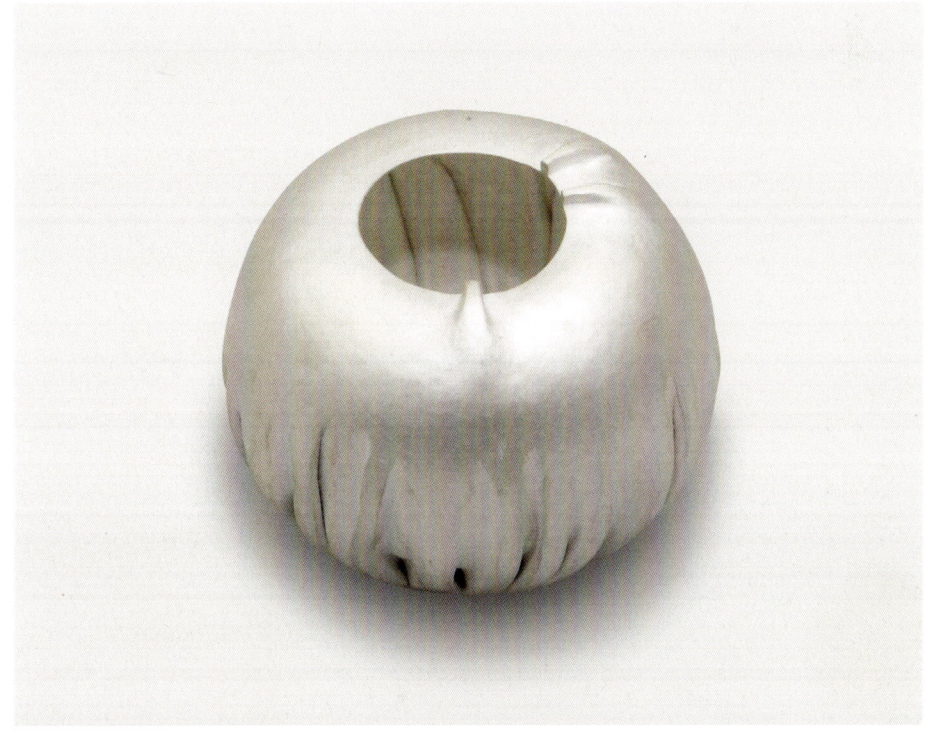

Sungho Cho

Objekt / Object — *Stacking of time 03*

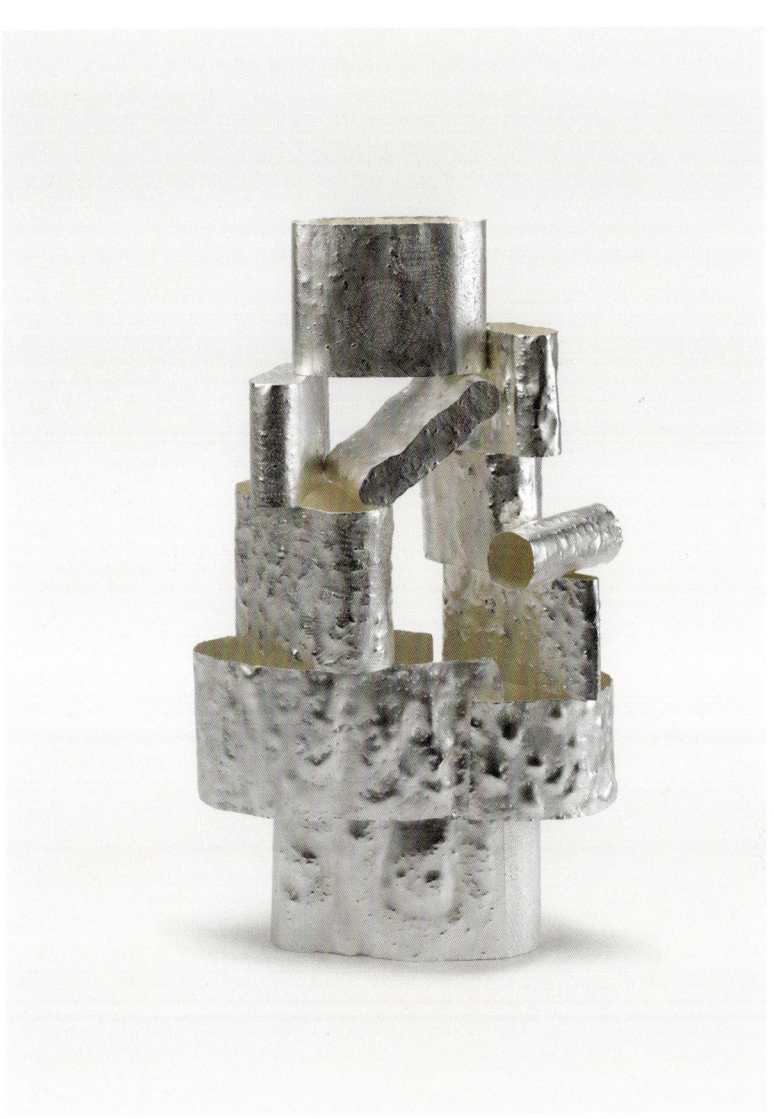

Sarah Cossham

Schale
Bowl

Ebbe & Flut

Vase

Pango

Andreas Decker

Vase *Roca*

Hanyi Feng•

Becher
Cups

DRINKAWARE

Gretal Ferguson

Objekt
Object

Escape Artist

Benedikt
Förster-Heyne

Becher *des wassers*
Cup *sanftheit...*

Andreas Frank

Besteck
Cutlery

NEUE GRIFFE –
NEU GEGOSSEN

101

Andreas
Frank

Vorlegebesteck
Serving cutlery

NEUE GRIFFE –
NEU GEGOSSEN

103

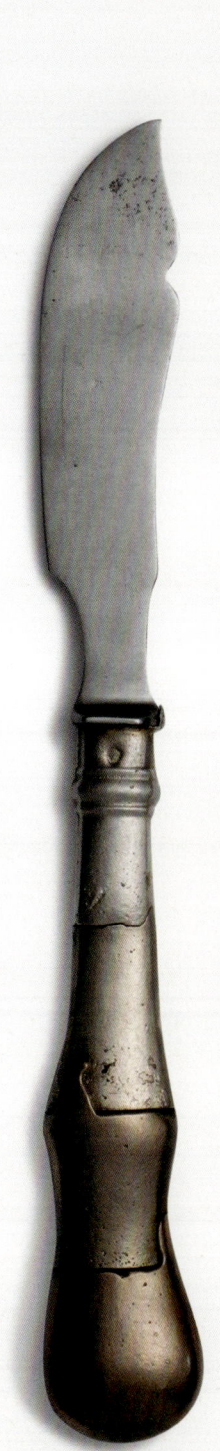

Luise
Fritzsche•

Teekanne
Teapot

Kristóf András Gelley

Teekanne
Teapot

*Kanne 2 –
»Jeiner Frühstück«*

Kirsten Haydon

Wandobjekt
Wall object

Ice Measures

Jiahn Hong•

Objekt
Object

Sonata

Marian Hosking

Laterne
Lantern

Shifting light swans on swamp vessel

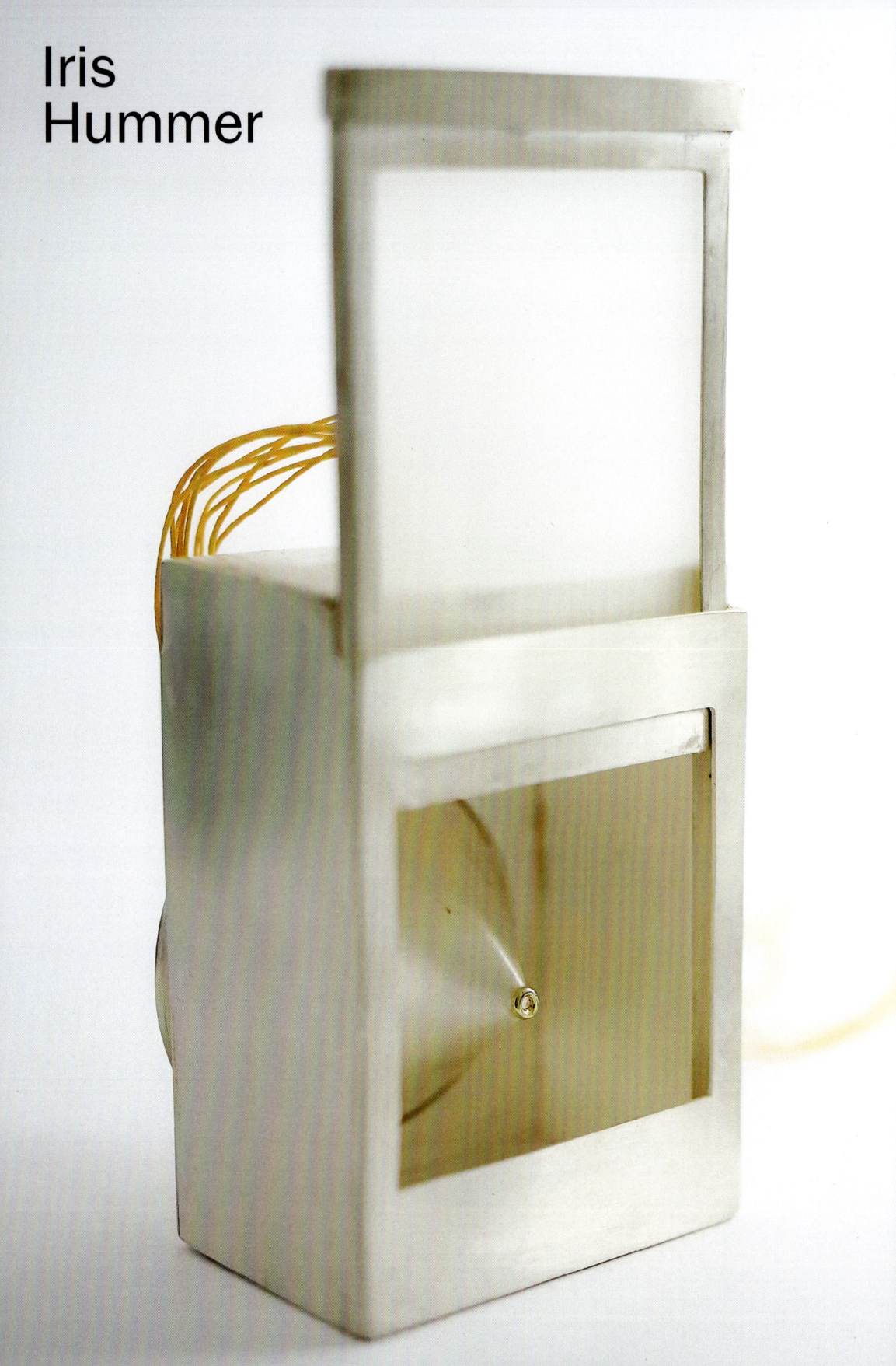

Iris
Hummer

Objekt
Object

Camera Obscura

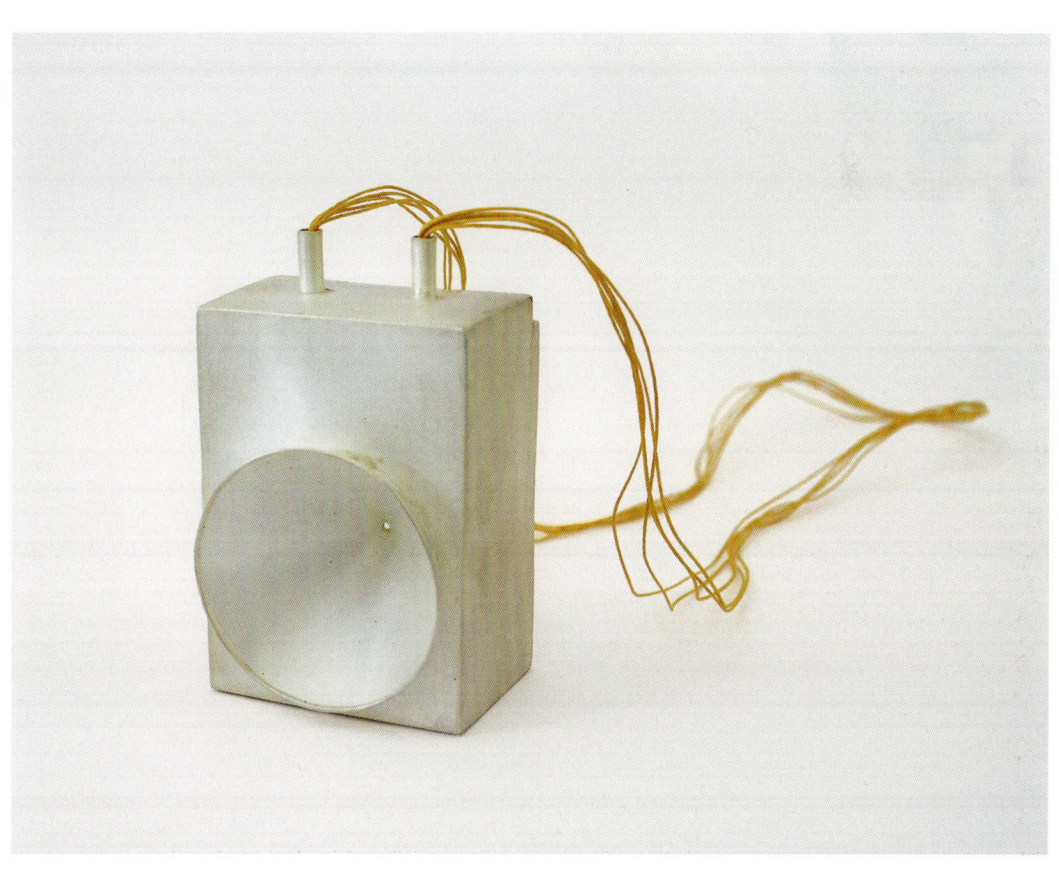

David Huycke

Wandobjekt
Wall object

Shiny Cloud

Inhwan Jeon

Objekt / Object

Taboo and Transgression

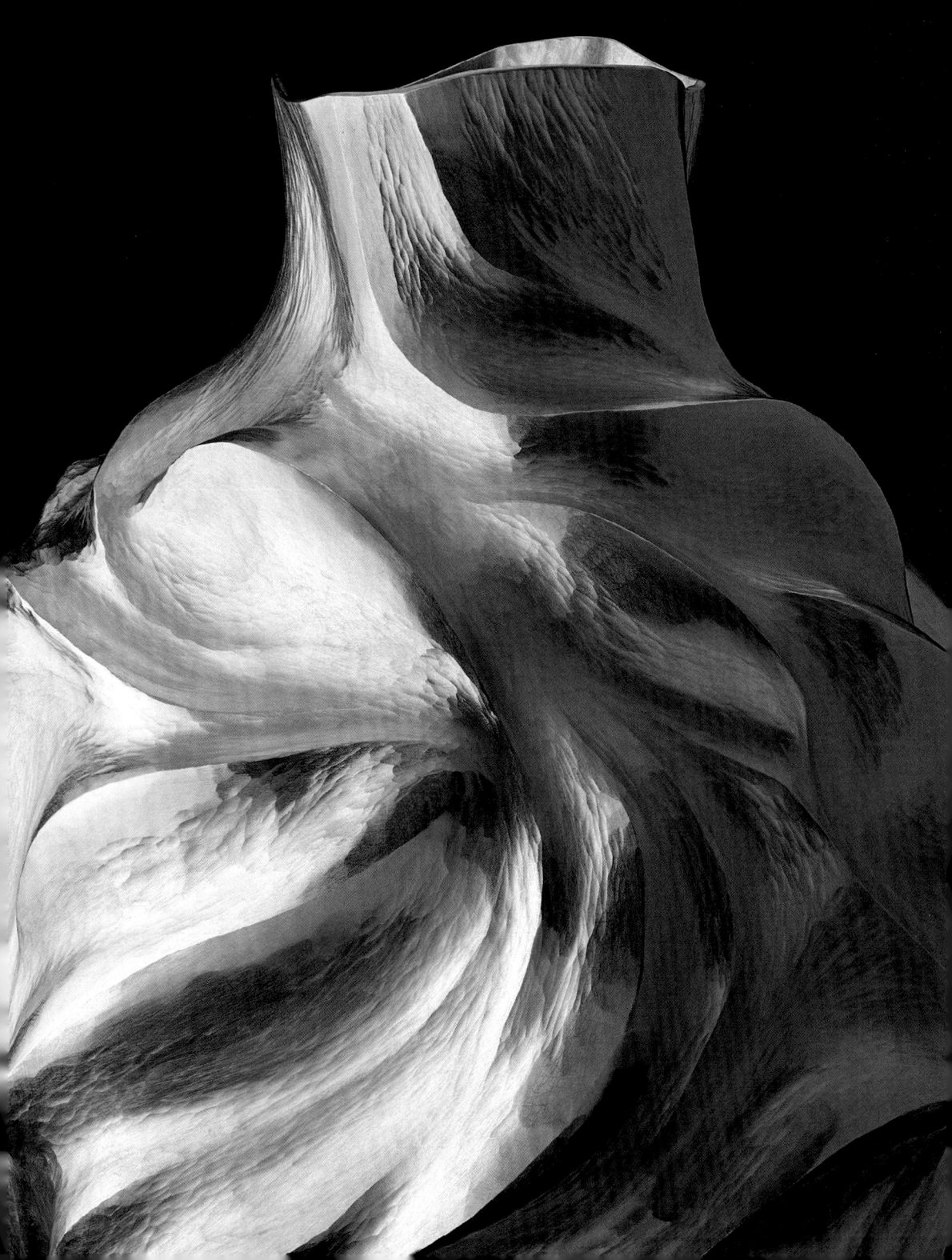

Vase

Routine Vase

Catherine Large

Gefäße
Vessels

Crumple

125

Annette Lechler

Objekt
Object

Schalenverkettung

Annette Lechler

Objekt
Object

Schalenverkettung
Quadrifolia

Zhizhong Li •

Objekte / Objects

Voiceless #1

Bo-Ting Lin

Kanne
Jug

*»happy moon kettle«
there is no any one
thing being with
earth! this is a moon
kettle! yes!*

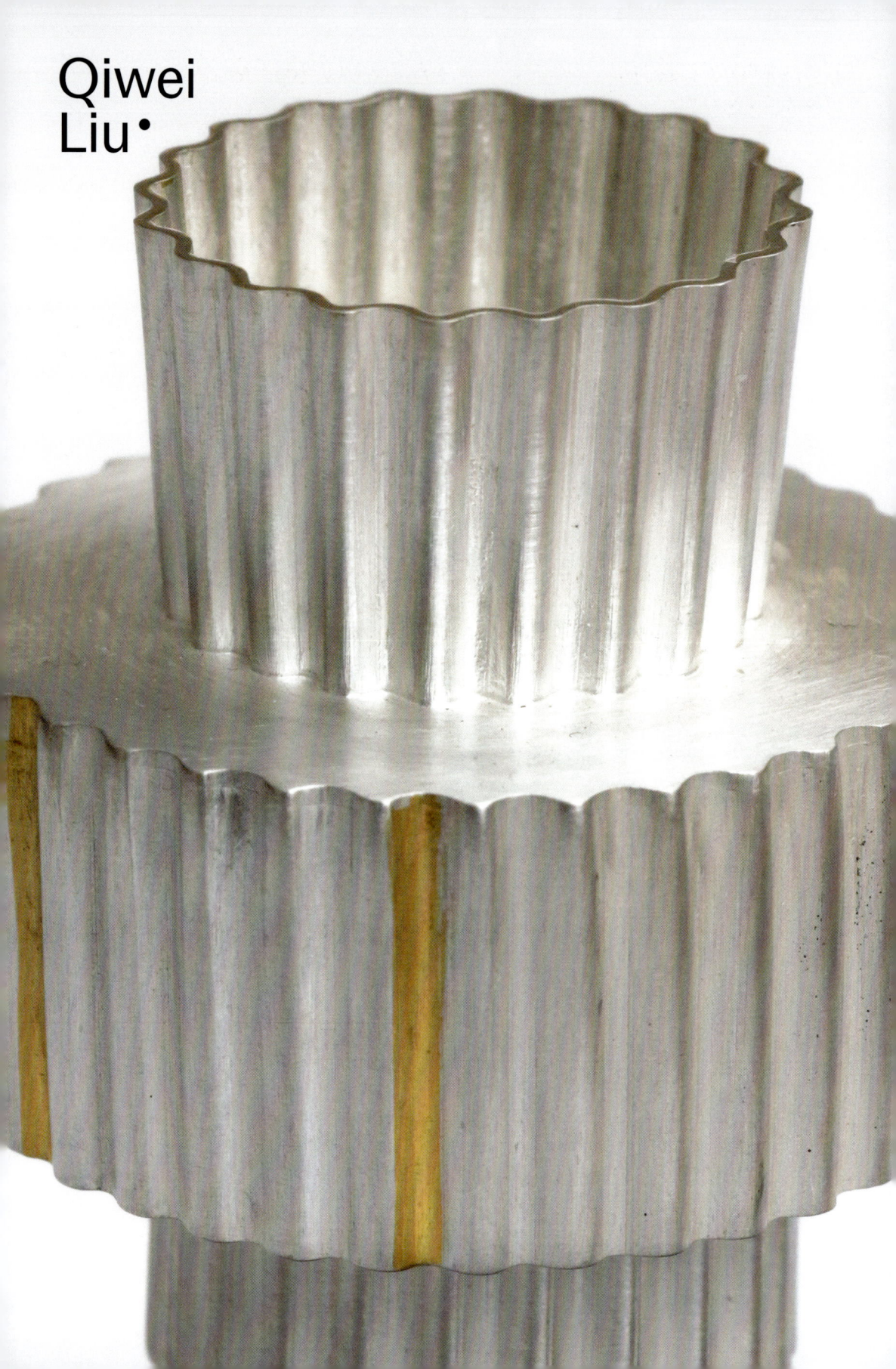

Qiwei Liu

Kerzenständer
Candlestick

Lithos Offering 1

Christine
Matthias

Objekt
Object

Militsa Milenkova & Callum Partridge•

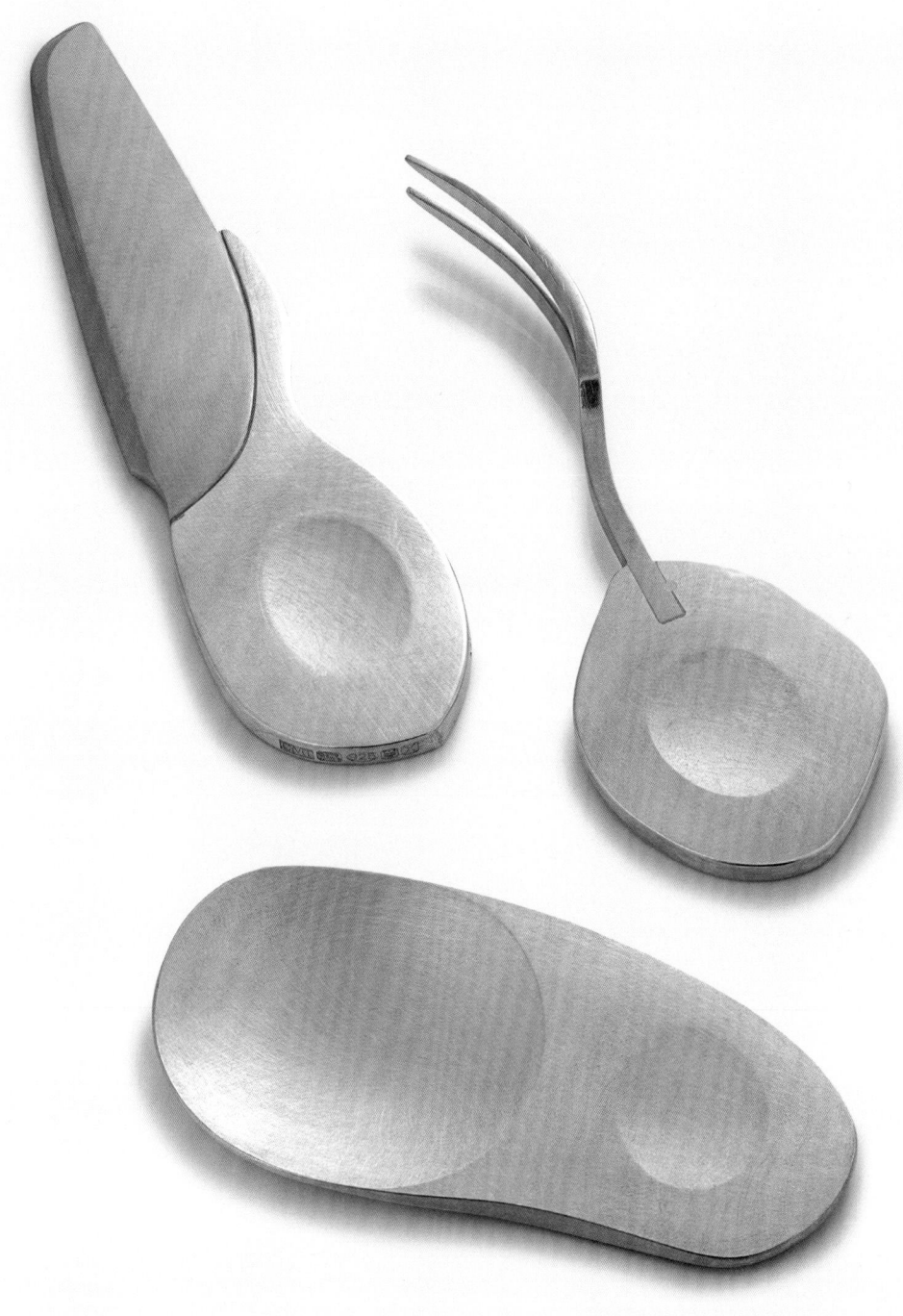

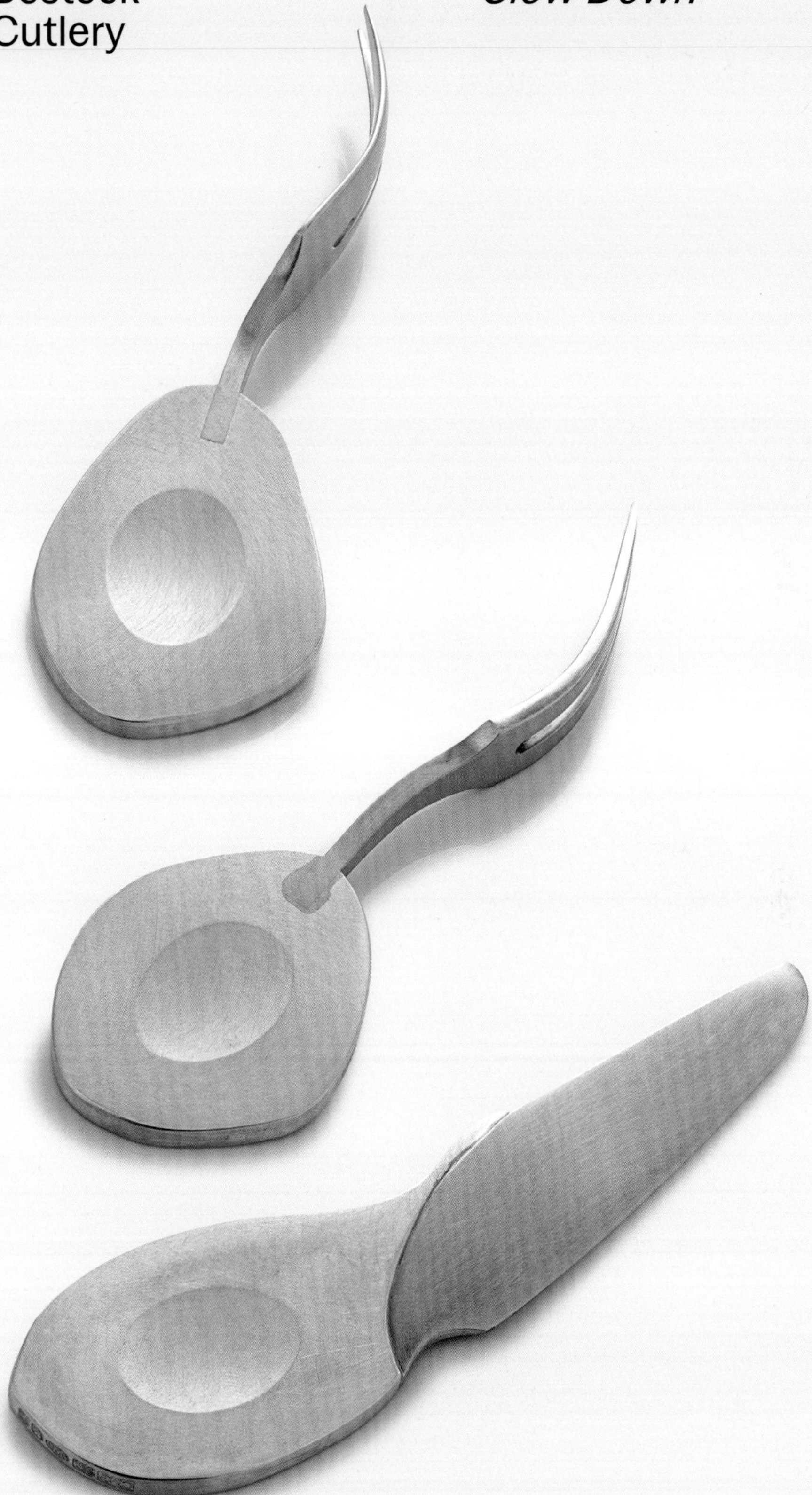

Besteck
Cutlery

Slow Down

139

Alex O'Connor

Karaffe und Becher
Carafe and cups

Equilibrium Vessel and Cups

141

Byungik
Park

Objekt
Object

소복소복
*(sobok sobok) –
The moment when
Heaven and Earth
connect*

Wu Peng•

Objekte
Objects

Stone Age

145

Christoph
Pilsel •

Teekanne
Teapot

Pearl

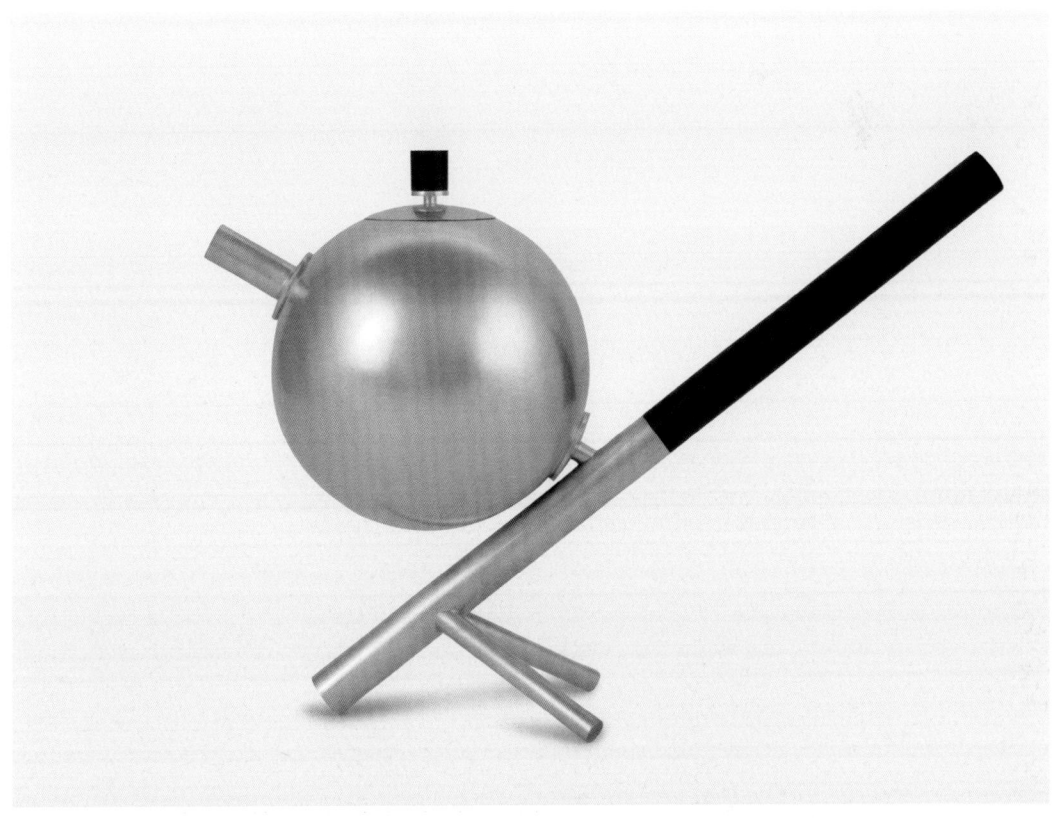

Christine
Ramel

Kaffeekanne
Coffee pot

Coffee pot

Yeunhee Ryu

Kanne
Jug

Goryeo

Helena Schepens

Besteck
Cutlery

Re-forging consumption

Juliane
Schölß

Gefäße
Vessels

Schwarze Gefäße

Gerrit
Schulze Raestrup •

Gefäß
Vessel

Tränengefäß 14

Regina Eva Sebold •

Altargerät
Altar implements

Vasa Sacra

Yegyu
Shin

Objekt
Object

Toy of Time II

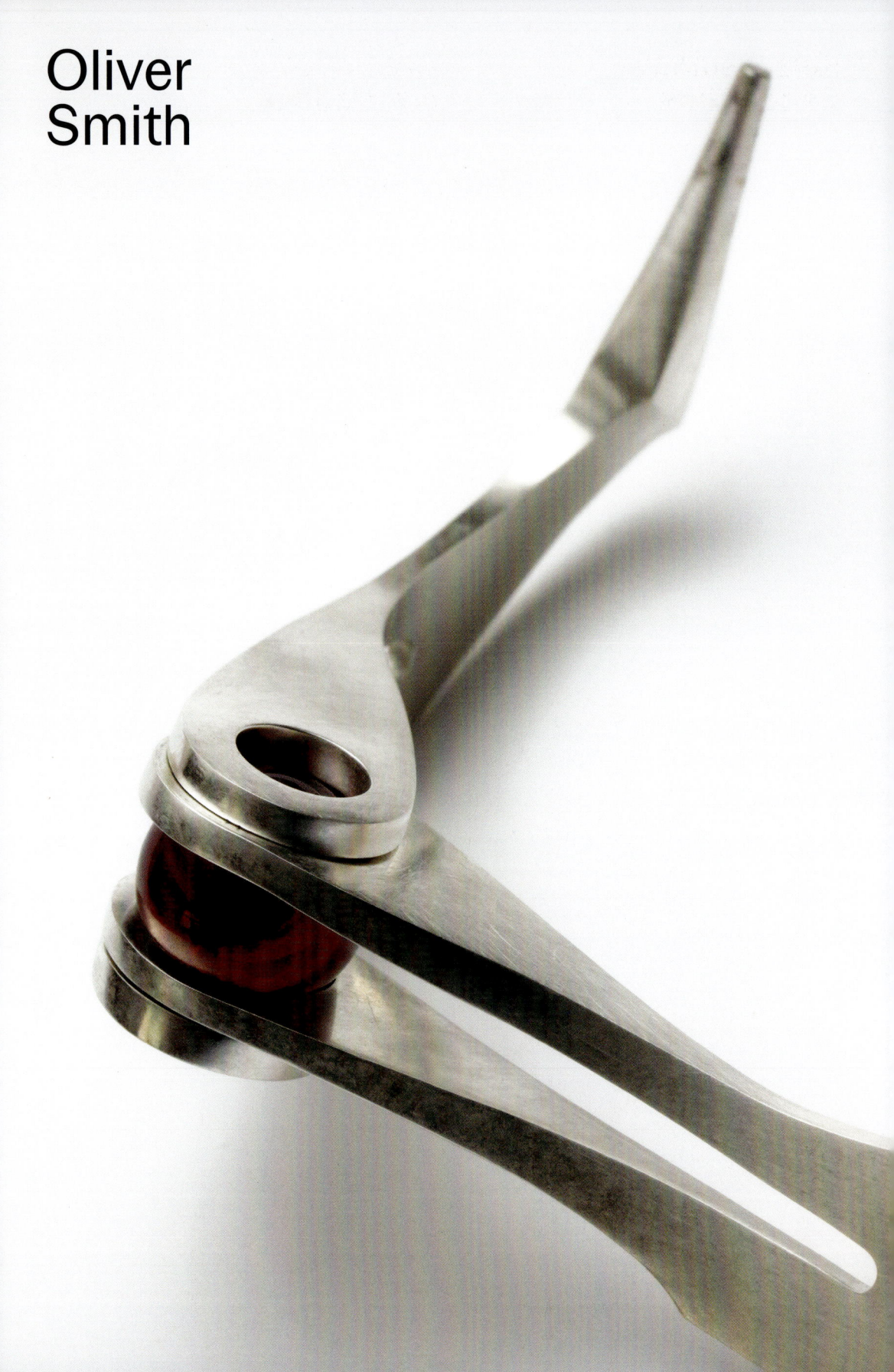

Oliver
Smith

Kerzenständer
Candlestick

Catenated
Candelabra

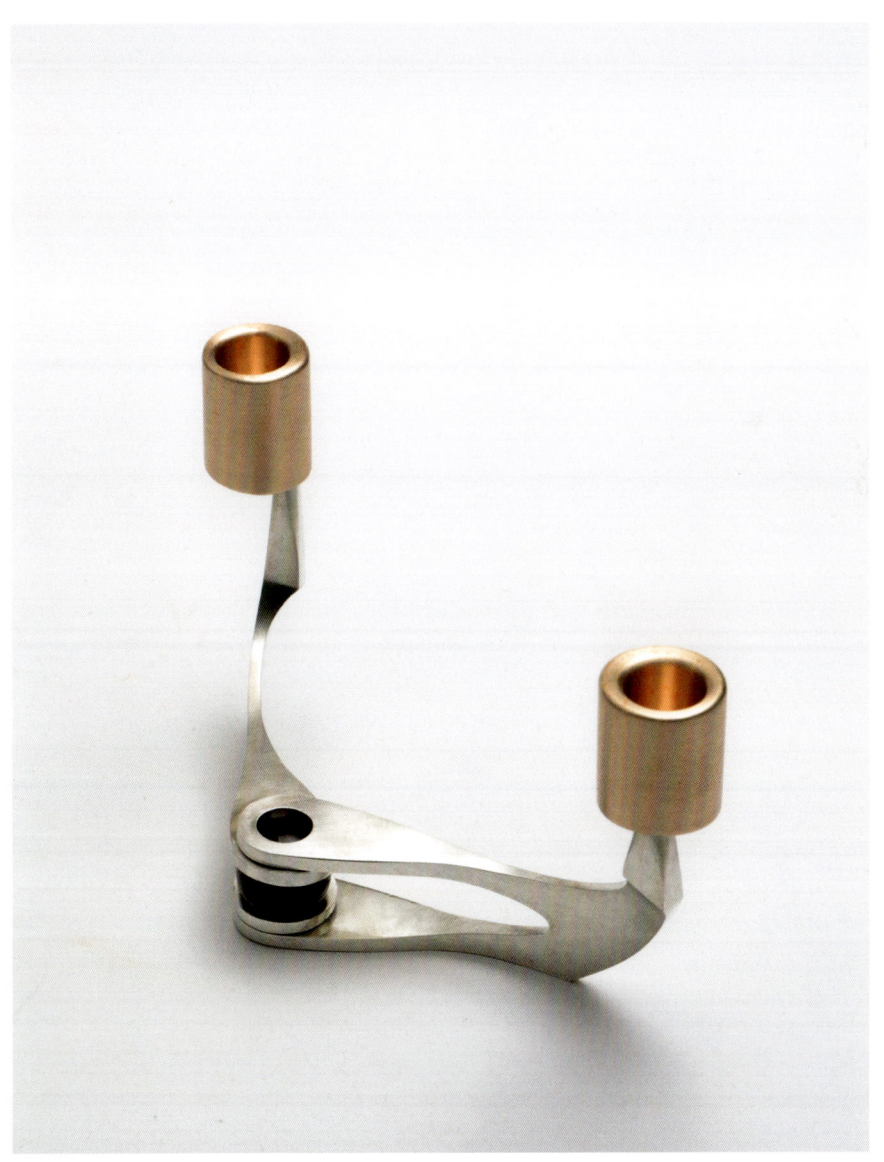

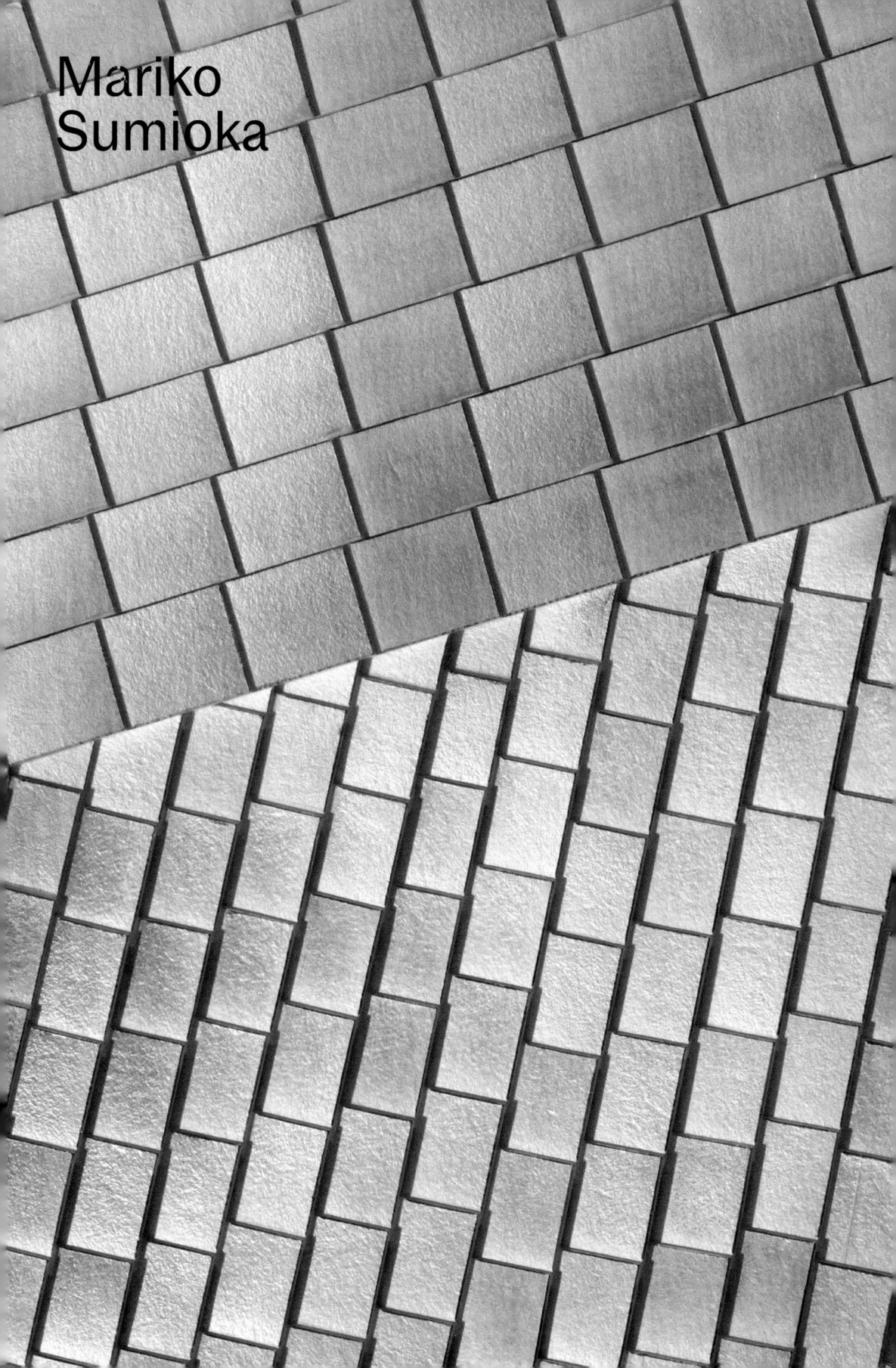

Dose
Box

Roof and roof

Lee
Sungyeoul

Flasche
Bottle

Bottle in Silver

Mohammad Taghavi

Karaffe
Carafe

Christoph
Weißhaar

Schale
Bowl

Investment #7

Tong Wu •

Besteck
Cutlery

Crown

Tong Wu

Objekt
Object

Liberation of Gemstone

175

Werkverzeichnis
List of Works

Farah Abdelhamid — 61
Objekt
Object
Bi-form 1
2024
Kupfer, versilbert, Glas. Aufgezogen, geschmiedet
Copper, silver-plated, glass. Raised, forged
16 × 7 × 8,5 cm

Eckhard Adler — 63
Teekanne
Teapot
Teekanne
2024
925/000 Silber, Holz. Montiert
925/000 silver, wood. Mounted
23 × 22 × 12,5 cm

Min Sick Ahn — 65
Kessel
Kettle
Silver Kettle 2023
2023
925/000 Silber, Edelstahl. Geschmiedet
925/000 silver, stainless steel. Forged
17 × 16 × 13 cm

Ana Albuquerque — 67
Objekt
Object
restart
2023
999/000 Silber, Textil. Laminiert, gedrückt, gestreckt. Auf dem Kopf tragbar
999/000 silver, textile. Laminated, bruised, stretched. Wearable on the head
18,5 × 31,5 × 23 cm

Barbara Amstutz — 69
Karaffe
Carafe
Karaffe 2024
2024
925/000 Silber. Getrieben, montiert, geätzt
925/000 silver. Chased, mounted, etched
26 × 8,5 × 7,5 cm

Ralf Auerbach — 71
Schale
Bowl
Schale 160
2023
Silber, Eisen. Aufgezogen, planiert. Doppelwandig
Silver, iron. Raised, planished. Double-walled
H 6,4 cm, ø 18,5 cm

Hyun Baek — 73
Vase
Timespace vase
2024
958/000 Silber. Geschmiedet, getrieben
958/000 silver. Forged, chased
35 × 20 × 11 cm

Eva Bauer — 75
Studie
Study
Goldi
2022
925/000 Silber, Kautschuk. Aufgezogen, montiert
925/000 silver, caoutchouc. Raised, mounted
Bis zu/up to 5 × 5 × 6 cm

Rebecca Bierbrodt — 57
Gefäß
Vessel
Angst
2023
999/000 Silber, 925/000 Silberdraht, geschwärzt. Aufgezogen, planiert, Draht gewickelt
999/000 silver, 925/000 silverwire, blackened. Raised, planished, wire spun
21 × 11 × 12 cm

Gitte Bjørn — 77
Urne
Urn
Anywhere Else
2022
Silber, Leder. Griff gestickt, silbergeschmiedet, getrieben, graviert, gegossene Details
Silver, leather. Handle stitched, forged in silver, chased, engraved, cast details
29 × 18 × 14 cm

Emil Borregaard — 79
Schale
Bowl
Giffelfad
2024
925/000 Silber. Geschmiedet
925/000 silver. Forged
4 × 37 × 12 cm

Tabea Helena Maki Brindöpke — 81
Milchkanne
Milk jug
Coffee & Games
2024
Tombak, Kupfer, versilbert. Aufgezogen, gepresst, montiert
Tombac, copper, silver-plated. Raised, pressed, mounted
13 × 12 × 12 cm

Ya-Ping Cheng — 83
Vase
2023
Silber. Aufgezogen
Silver. Raised
6,5 × 6,5 × 3,6 cm

Ya-Ping Cheng — 85
Vase
2024
Silber. Aufgezogen
Silver. Raised
5,5 × 5,5 × 4,2 cm

Sungho Cho — 87
Objekt
Object
Stacking of time 03
2023
925/000 Silber. Wachsausgussverfahren, gelötet
925/000 silver. Wax-rubbed, melt-drawn, cast, soldered
46 × 28 × 14 cm

Sarah Cossham — 89
Schale
Bowl
Ebbe & Flut
2024
925/000 Silber, 200 ct. Rubine. Gegossen
925/000 silver, 200 ct. rubies. Cast
H 7 cm, ø 18 cm

Andreas Decker — 91
Vase
Pango
2024
925/000 Silber. Geschmiedet, montiert, teils geschliffen, teils geschwärzt
925/000 silver. Forged, mounted, partly polished, partly blackened
H 25 cm, ø 15 cm

Andreas Decker 93
Vase
Roca
2024
925/000 Silber. Geschmiedet, montiert, teils geschliffen
925/000 silver. Forged, mounted, partly polished
H 30 cm, ø 11 cm

Hanyi Feng 95
Becher
Cups
DRINKAWARE
2023
Messing, versilbert. Gepresst, gelötet, gefaltet
Brass, silver-plated. Pressed, soldered, folded
6,5 × 6 × 10 cm

Gretal Ferguson 97
Objekt
Object
Escape Artist
2024
950/000 Silber. Aufgezogen, gelötet
950/000 silver. Raised, soldered
Bis zu/up to 9 × 15 × 8 cm

Benedikt Förster-Heyne 99
Becher
Cup
des wassers sanftheit...
2024
925/000 Silber. Geschmiedet, getrieben, zieseliert, montiert
925/000 silver. Forged, chased, chiseled, mounted
H 11,3 cm, ø 6,8 cm

Andreas Frank 101
Besteck
Cutlery
NEUE GRIFFE – NEU GEGOSSEN
2024
925/000 Silber, Bronze, Messing. Sandgussverfahren
925/000 silver, bronze, brass. Sand-cast
Bis zu/up to 20 × 2 × 1 cm

Andreas Frank 103
Vorlegebesteck
Serving cutlery
NEUE GRIFFE – NEU GEGOSSEN
2024
925/000 Silber, verschiedene Bronze- und Silberlegierungen. Sandgussverfahren
925/000 silver, different bronze and silver alloys. Sand-cast
Bis zu/up to 24 × 3 × 1,5 cm

Luise Fritzsche 105
Teekanne
Teapot
2024
925/000 Silber, Walnussfurnier. Montiert
925/000 silver, walnut veneer. Mounted
19,5 × 18,5 × 11,5 cm

Kristóf András Gelley 107
Teekanne
Teapot
Kanne 2 – »Jeiner Frühstück«
2024
925/000 Silber, Stahl. Aufgezogen, getieft, planiert, gelötet
925/000 silver, steel. Raised, sunk, planished, soldered
19 × 22 × 16,3 cm

Kirsten Haydon 109
Wandobjekt
Wall object
Ice Measures
2024
Silber, Kupfer, Shibuichi, Emaille, Reflektor-Perlen, Destillations-Kugeln, Fototransfer, Stahl. Aufgezogen, gegossen, Oberflächenbehandlung, emailliert
Silver, copper, Shibuichi, enamel, reflector beads, distillation spheres, photo transfer, steel. Raised, cast, surface treatment, enameled
Gesamt/total 33,5 × 125,5 × 18 cm

Jiahn Hong 111
Objekt
Object
Sonata
2024
950/000 Silber, ABS
950/000 silver, ABS
19,5 × 7,5 × 24,7 cm

Marian Hosking 113
Laterne
Lantern
Shifting light swans on swamp vessel
2024
925/000 Silber, Sassafras-Holz. Gebohrt, geformt, genietet
925/000 silver, Sassafras timber. Drilled, formed, rivetted
H 31,5 cm, ø 17 cm

Iris Hummer 115
Objekt
Object
Camera Obscura
2024
925/000 Silber, 585/000 Gold, Bergkristall, Leinenschnur. Gezogen, gebogen, zusammengesetzt
925/000 silver, 585/000 gold, rock crystal, linen cord. Drawn, bent, assembled
Bis zu/up to 8,7 × 5,5 × 4,3 cm

David Huycke 117
Wandobjekt
Wall object
Shiny Cloud
2024
925/000 Silber. Geformt, gelötet, poliert
925/000 silver. Formed, soldered, polished
17,5 × 31,5 × 10,5 cm

Inhwan Jeon 119
Objekt
Object
Taboo and Transgression
2024
999/000 Silber, 925/000 Silber. Geformt, aufgezogen, geschweißt, gelötet
999/000 silver, 925/000 silver. Formed, raised, welded, soldered
13 × 13 × 18 cm

Yong-il Jeon 39
Teekanne
Teapot
Tea pot with a nickel handle
2024
925/000 Silber, Nickel. Aufgezogen, gefertigt, zusammengesetzt
925/000 silver, nickel. Raised, fabricated, assembled
20 × 23 × 13 cm

Jae Hui Jeong 51
Schale
Bowl
Conceal and Reveal
2024
999/000 Silber. Gehämmert
999/000 silver. Hammered
13,5 × 24,5 × 24,5 cm

Carl Kankowsky 53
Kanne
Jug
2024
925/000 Silber. Montiert
925/000 silver. Mounted
20 × 10 × 12 cm

Sang Hoon Kim 121
Vase
Anecdote Vase
2024
999/000 Silber. Gehämmert, getrieben
999/000 silver. Hammered, chased
21 × 21 × 26,5 cm

Sang Hoon Kim 123
Vase
Routine Vase
2024
999/000 Silber, Ottchil. Gehämmert, getrieben
999/000 silver, Ottchil. Hammered, chased
13 × 15 × 19 cm

Catherine Large 125
Gefäße
Vessels
Crumple
2024
999/000 Silber, Emaille. Getieft, aufgezogen, gefaltet, getrieben, emailliert
999/000 silver, enamel. Sunk, raised, folded, chased, enameled
Bis zu/up to 4,5 × 6 × 6 cm

Annette Lechler 127
Objekt
Object
Schalenverkettung
2024
925/000 Silber. Kalte Verformung. Veränderbar
925/000 silver. Cold-formed. Changeable
2 × 15 × 12 cm

Annette Lechler 129
Objekt
Object
Schalenverkettung Quadrifolia
2023
925/000 Silber. Kalte Verformung. Veränderbar
925/000 silver. Cold-formed. Changeable
H 4 cm, Ø 16 cm

Zhizhong Li 131
Objekte
Objects
Voiceless #1
2024
999/000 Silber. Aufgezogen, gefaltet
999/000 silver. Raised, folded
Bis zu/up to 16 × 12 × 12 cm

Bo-Ting Lin 133
Kanne
Jug
»happy moon kettle« there is no any one thing being with earth! this is a moon kettle! yes!
2024
999/000 Silber. Aufgezogen, geprägt, getrieben, poliert
999/000 silver. Raised, embossed, chased, polished
21 × 17 × 16 cm

Qiwei Liu 135
Kerzenständer
Candlestick
Lithos Offering 1
2024
Silber, 24k Blattgold, Emaille. Gelötet, Keum-boo
Silver, 24k gold foil, enamel. Soldered, Keum-boo
12 × 15 × 15 cm

Christine Matthias 137
Objekt
Object
2024
Silber. Beweglich montiert. Veränderbar
Silver. Mounted foldable. Changeable
Bis zu/up to 1 × 18 × 20 cm

Militsa Milenkova & Callum Partridge 139
Besteck
Cutlery
Slow Down
2022
925/000 Silber, Edelstahl. Durchbrochen, gefüllt, geschmiedet, lasergelötet, geschmirgelt
925/000 silver, stainless steel. Pierced, filled, forged, laser-welded, sanded
Bis zu/up to 12 × 3,5 × 0,4 cm

Alex O'Connor 141
Karaffe und Becher
Carafe and cups
Equilibrium Vessel and Cups
2023
925/000 Silber. Gedreht, gefertigt, getrieben
925/000 silver. Spun, fabricated, chased
Bis zu/up to 25 cm, Ø 10,5 cm

Byungik Park 143
Objekt
Object
소복소복 *(sobok sobok) – The moment when Heaven and Earth connect*
2024
960/000 Silber. Geschweißt, gelötet
960/000 silver. Welded, soldered
11 × 11 × 51 cm

Jieun Park 41
Gefäß
Vessel
The flexible vessel 2372
2024
925/000 Silber, Leinenfaden. Geschmiedet, gewebt
925/000 silver, linen thread. Forged, woven
14 × 11 × 11,5 cm

Wu Peng 145
Objekte
Objects
Stone Age
2024
Silber, Kupfer. Mokume-Gane, gehämmert
Silver, copper. Mokume-gane, hammered
Bis zu/up to 9 × 16,5 × 12 cm

Christoph Pilsel 147
Teekanne
Teapot
Pearl
2024
Silber, Grenadill-Holz. Aufgezogen
Silver, African blackwood. Raised
22 × 31 × 13 cm

Christine Ramel 149
Kaffeekanne
Coffee pot
Coffee pot
2024
Silber, Glas. Geschmiedet
Silver, glass. Forged
36,5 × 15,5 × 12,5 cm

Yeunhee Ryu 35
Kanne
Jug
Goryeo 2
2023
925/000 Silber.
Geschmiedet
925/000 silver. Forged
22 × 15 × 10 cm

Yeunhee Ryu 151
Kanne
Jug
Goryeo
2022
925/000 Silber, Stein.
Geschmiedet
925/000 silver, stone.
Forged
19,5 × 19 × 8 cm

Helena Schepens 153
Besteck
Cutlery
Re-forging consumption
2024
925/000 Silber, Muschel.
Aufgezogen, geschmiedet, gelötet, gegossen
925/000 silver, shell.
Raised, forged, soldered, cast
Bis zu/up to
20,5 × 6 × 3 cm

Juliane Schölß 155
Gefäße
Vessels
Schwarze Gefäße
2022
925/000 Silber. Montiert, geschwärzt
925/000 silver. Mounted, blackened
Bis zu/up to 36,4 cm,
Ø 10,5 cm

Gerrit Schulze Raestrup 157
Gefäß
Vessel
Tränengefäß 14
2024
Silber-Kupferlegierung, Salz. Gegossen, getaucht
Silver and copper alloy, salt. Cast, dipped
H 8 cm, Ø 6 cm

Regina Eva Sebold 159
Altargerät
Altar implements
Vasa Sacra
2023
925/000 Silber, Buchsbaum. Montiert, gedrechselt
925/000 silver, boc wood.
Mounted, primmed
Bis zu/up to 18 × 12 × 8 cm

Yegyu Shin 45
Objekt
Object
Toy of Time I
2024
925/000 Silber, Faden.
Transformierende Technik, genäht
925/000 silver, thread.
Transforming technology, sewn
28 × 5,5 × 4 cm

Yegyu Shin 161
Objekt
Object
Toy of Time II
2024
925/000 Silber, Faden.
Transformierende Technik, genäht
925/000 silver, thread.
Transforming technology, sewn
Bis zu/up to
18,5 × 4,2 × 1,2 cm

Oliver Smith 163
Kerzenständer
Candlestick
Catenated Candelabra
2024
900/000 Silber, synthetischer Rubin, Shibuichi, Monel. Gegossen, heißgeschmiedet, kaltgeschmiedet, angepasst, veredelt. Veränderbar
900/000 silver, synthetic ruby, Shibuichi, Monel.
Cast, hot-forged, cold-forged, fitted, finished.
Changeable
Bis zu/up to
13 × 24 × 3,5 cm

Mariko Sumioka 165
Dose
Box
Roof and roof
2024
970/000 Silber, 950/000 Silber. Montiert
970/000 silver, 950/000 silver. Mounted
4 × 14,8 × 9 cm

Lee Sungyeoul 167
Flasche
Bottle
Bottle in Silver
2023
925/000 Silber, Leder.
Geschmiedet
925/000 silver, leather.
Forged
8,5 × 8,5 × 32 cm

Mohammad Taghavi 169
Karaffe
Carafe
2024
925/000 Silber. Montiert
925/000 silver. Mounted
14 × 9 × 8 cm

Christoph Weißhaar 171
Schale
Bowl
Investment #7
2024
999/000 Silber. Gepresst
999/000 silver. Pressed
2,2 × 7,8 × 6 cm

Tong Wu 173
Besteck
Cutlery
Crown
2022
925/000 Silber.
3D-Design, 3D-gegossen, poliert
925/000 silver. 3D design, 3D cast, polished
Bis zu/up to 14 × 2 × 4 cm

Tong Wu 175
Objekt
Object
Liberation of Gemstone
2023
925/000 Silber, Glas.
3D-Design, Glasherstellung, poliert
925/000 silver, glass.
3D design, glassmaking, polished
H 9 cm, Ø 7,5 cm

Siqiu Zhang 47
Vase
shimmering
2024
999/000 Silber.
Filigranarbeit
999/000 silver. Filigree
16 × 15 × 19 cm

Farah Abdelhamid

1992
lives in Cairo EG

Born in Vienna, Farah has been moving around the world since she was 30 days old, having now lived in 9 countries and attended over 13 schools, Egypt is home.

Farah graduated from the prestigious Rhode Island School of Design in 2015 with a BFA in Jewelry and Metalsmithing, and will receive her MA in Product Design in Germany in March 2025, she is currently a guest student at the HAWK in Hildesheim working under Prof. Melanie Isverding on her Master's thesis.

As a founder of FforFarah Contemporary Jewelry, her jewelry studio practice in Cairo, Farah is also an interdisciplinary artist, maker, teacher, and writer always forging new visions and perspectives to her work and ethos: investigating the relationship between body and object.

In her obsession with hollow vessels, and a passionate maker of material, Farah was mesmerized by the world of glass flame-working and has shifted her practice and studies to incorporating it with metal raising and forging. This allows her to also work on a larger scale and to larger discoveries about perception, the senses, and craft techniques.

Farah used to work from her old Cairo studio for seven years until it was demolished in September 2023 due to construction in the area, and thus has taken this opportunity as an open ticket to explore craft communities and opportunities around the world.

@fforfarah
www.fforfarah.com

Eckhard Adler

1948
lebt in Hanau DE
und Santanyí ES

1966 Gesellenprüfung als Gold- und Silberschmied
1969–1972 Staatliche Zeichenakademie Hanau
1971 Meisterprüfung im Goldschmiedehandwerk
• Staatlich geprüfter Gestalter für Schmuck und Gerät
1972–1975 FHG Pforzheim (Prof. Reinhold Reiling)
1975 Dipl. Designer (FH)
1975–1980 Freie Kunst, HBK Braunschweig (Prof. Malte Sartorius und Prof. Gerhard Büttenbender)
1981–1982 Studienreferendar
1983–1985 Kunstpädagoge
1985 Lehrer für Schmuckgestaltung und Goldschmieden, Staatliche Zeichenakademie Hanau
1988–2008 Studiendirektor, Abteilungsleiter für den Fachbereich Gestaltung, Leitung einer Fachklasse für Schmuckgestaltung, Staatliche Zeichenakademie Hanau
seit 2008 freischaffender Künstler und Goldschmied

@eckhardadler
www.eckhard-adler.de
www.goldschmiedekurse-mallorca.de

Min Sick Ahn

1969
lives in Seoul KR

Throughout my academic journey, I developed technical expertise in metalcraft and an aesthetic sense for form, focusing on creating functional yet sculptural pieces. While studying at the AdBK in Nuremberg, I specialized in silversmithing, primarily working with silver for tableware. Using traditional forging methods, I also explored complementary materials like rosewood and ebony. My goal has always been to highlight silver's unique material qualities – its hue, structure, and practicality. Inspired by the harmony between humanity and nature through the changing seasons, I extract design motifs to craft functional yet beautiful silverware. Each piece is designed with an individual in mind, resulting in one-of-a-kind objects that embody artistic perfection. Though functional, my works also achieve sculptural excellence. The beauty of silverware is enhanced when serving food, driving my dedication to blending practical function with artistic expression in my creations. I aim to merge aesthetic form with practicality in every piece I design.

Solo Exhibitions
2005 Kyungin Museum of Fine Art, Seoul
2008 KCDF, Seoul

Group Exhibitions
2014 *Korea Craft Exhibition* Archaeological Museum Red Fort, New Delhi
2020 *Water that Awakens One's Senses* Seoul
2022 *20th Silver Triennial International*

www.auagmetalcraft.com

Ana Albuquerque

1964
lives in Carcavelos PT

1984–1987 Applied Arts, Fundação Ricardo Espírito Santo Silva
1988–1994 Sculptor, University of Fine Arts Lisbon
1989–1992 ar.co, Jewelry and Contacto Direto, Lisbon
1992 Worked in the studio of jewelry maker Nunes Garrido
2007–2010 Vice President of PIN Associação Portuguesa de Joalharia Contemporânea
2008–2023 Teacher, ar.co, Lisbon

Solo Exhibitions
2008 *Decotes Décolletage* Museu Nacional do Traje, Lisbon
2011 *Border City: Tallinn – Lisbon ARRIVAL – DEPARTURE* Tallin

Group Exhibitions
2011 *European Triennial for Contemporary Jewellery* Mons
2013 *Beijing International Art Biennale, Jewelry _Identity* Beijing
2021 *1a Bienal de Joalharia Contemporânea* Lisbon
• *Cold Sweat* Museu de S. Roque, Lisbon

Barbara Amstutz
1970
lebt in Oberwil CH

1988–1992 Studium der Geschichte, Philosophie und Vergleichenden Religionswissenschaften in Jerusalem und Basel
1995–1999 Goldschmiedelehre in Basel
• Ausbildung in Tiefdruck/Radieren an der Schule für Gestaltung Basel
1999–2003 Arbeit als Goldschmiedin in Carouge, Genf und Basel
• Arbeitsaufenthalt (Radieren/Illustration) in Sofia
2003–05 Ausbildung zur Silberschmiedin in Schoonhoven
seit 2006 freischaffende Silberschmiedin in der Region Basel

Auszeichnungen
1999 *Prix Golay Buchel* Uhren- und Schmuckmesse, Basel
2003–2005 Stipendium E. E. Zunft zu Hausgenossen, Basel
2014 *Prix Jumelles*, *L'intelligence de la main*
2022 Stadtgoldschmiedin Schwäbisch Gmünd

Einzelausstellungen
2013 *Müstair – Schalenobjekte* Museum Kloster St. Johann, Müstair
2019 *Barbara Amstutz Orfèvre* Galerie Latham, Genf
2022 *Texturen* Kulturzentrum Prediger Schwäbisch Gmünd

Gruppenausstellungen
2015 *Silber & Gold* Historisches Museum Basel
2017 *Tresor Contemporary Craft* Messe Basel
2018 *Homo Faber* Fondazione Giorgio Cini, Venedig
2020 *Friedrich Becker Preis* Düsseldorf, Hanau
2021 *Prix Européen des Arts Appliqués (BeCraft)*, Mons
2022 Galerie Latham, Brafa Art Fair, Brüssel
2024 *résonance[s]*, Salon européen des métiers d'art, Straßburg

Arbeiten in öffentlichen Sammlungen
• Historisches Museum Basel
• Museum für Kunst und Kulturgeschichte, Dortmund
• Rehmann-Museum, Laufenburg
• Musée d'art et d'histoire, Neuchâtel
• Schweizerisches Nationalmuseum, Zürich

www.barbaraamstutz.ch

Ralf Auerbach
1964
lebt in Flieden DE

1980–1983 Lehre als Schlosser und Kunstschmied in Fulda
1985–1988 Ausbildung zum Silberschmied, Staatliche Zeichenakademie Hanau
1988–1990 Wanderjahre und Gesellenzeit: Allan Scharff, Kopenhagen, Stefan Epp, Insel Reichenau, Hendrik Forster, Australien
1990–1992 Meisterprüfung Silberschmied, staatlich geprüfter Gestalter, Fachschule, Staatliche Zeichenakademie Hanau
1995–2007 Werkstatt in Fulda
2014–2024 Entwurfs- und Design-Arbeit für Ravissant Siver, New Delhi
seit 2007 Werkstatt in Flieden

@auerbachsilversmith
www.auerbach-silberschmied.de

Hyun Baek
1988
lives in Goyang KR

Baek Hyun got his MFA and BFA degrees in Metal Craft from Kookmin University from 2008 to 2015. He wrote a thesis on visualizing the properties of time and continued his artistic activities by researching time, space, object forms, and surface textures. After graduating, he trained in hammering while working at William Lee's workshop and began creating silverware. In 2018, he received a working holiday visa and completed a program in Bishopsland Educational Trust, England. He won awards at the *Goldsmiths' Craft & Design Council Awards* in 2020 and spent two years working in Great Britain before returning to Korea. Since then, he has been developing his artistic world, participating in two solo exhibitions as well as several group exhibitions and fairs. He is currently teaching students at Sungshin Women's University, Wonkwang University, and Daegu Catholic University.

@hbmaking

Eva Bauer
1979
lebt in Hanau DE

2000–2003 Bildkunst Akademie Hamburg (Buchillustration)
2004–2008 Ausbildung zur Silberschmiedin, Staatliche Zeichenakademie Hanau
2007 Gründung des Forums für Gold und Silber, Hanau
2008 freischaffende und projektbezogene Arbeit, Silberschmiede Micha Peteler, Köln
seit 2009 Atelier und Galerie, Hanau
seit 2017 Atelier/Galerie Villa Masch, Hanau

Auszeichnungen
2008 1. Preis *Schale der Lüste* 's-Hertogenbosch
2009 Anerkennungspreis *Jewellery of India* Hanau
2012 Anerkennungspreis *Silber bewegt* Grassi Museum, Leipzig
2016 Anerkennungspreis, Silver Festival Legnica

Arbeiten in öffentlichen Sammlungen
Badisches Landesmuseum, Karlsruhe

@forumobjektgestaltung.de
www.evagold-art.de

Rebecca Bierbrodt
2000
lebt in Hanau DE

2020–2024 Ausbildung zur Silberschmiedin, Staatliche Zeichenakademie Hanau
seit 2024 Anschlusslehre zur Graveurin

@bie.re

Gitte Bjørn

1965
lives in Copenhagen DK

Gitte Bjørn is a trained goldsmith, whose curiosity concerning her art and craft seems to be never-ending. With over 30 years of professional work, she has moved through small jewellery and silver hollowware to large bronze sculptures and architectural assignments solved in close collaboration with established design studios.

Gitte's idiom is always narrative and often filled with humour. She works very thematically and has held five large thematic solo exhibitions across the years. The 2009 *Neither Fish nor Fowl* and 2015 *Body & Soul* silver hollowware exhibitions were held at the official Danish silverware museum Koldinghus. In 2023 her jewellery solo exhibition *TAPAS* was shown to record crowds at Design Museum Denmark.

@gittebjorn
www.gittebjorn.dk

Emil Borregaard

1987
lives in Virum DK

2008–2012 Apprenticeship as silversmith, Georg Jensen A/S
2008–2018 Silversmith, Georg Jensen A/S
since 2012 Self-employed
2016–2017 Alexandre School for optical diamond setting, Professional Stone Setting, Diploma (Alexander Sidorov)
2017 Private lessons from metal artist Kazuo Kashima, Japan

Awards
2012 ML-award (*Metalindustriens Lærlingepris*)
• *The Silver Medal* from Goldsmith Guild
2013 *The Honorary Medal* from the Association of Craftsmen in Copenhagen (Haandværkerforeningen i Kjøbenhavn)

@borregaard_brothers
www.borregaardbrothers.com

Tabea Helena Maki Brindöpke

2001
lebt in Hanau DE

2020–2024 Ausbildung zur Goldschmiedin, Staatliche Zeichenakademie Hanau
seit 2024 Ausbildung zur Silberschmiedin, Staatliche Zeichenakademie Hanau

Ya-Ping Cheng

1992
lives in New Taipei City TW

Cheng graduated from the National Taiwan University of Arts, majoring in Craft Creation.

Sungho Cho

1975
lives in Cheongju KR

I have been dedicated to the activities crossing boundaries between forms and materials of jewelry and objects. I majored in Metal Craft at Seoul National University before studying at Alchimia in Florence and AdBK in Munich. Staying in Europe, I began to produce experimental and highly refined jewelry conceived from the trends in contemporary Europe. My works in this period are represented by the items made by recycling industrial products, such as credit cards and Lego bricks, reflecting an aspect of the modern society in a symbolic manner. I have begun to expand my artwork to metal objects using soft wax-based precision casting process. I created thin objects up to 0.7 mm-thick, capturing surface textures with a variety of texturing techniques, such as stamping and drawing.

I have recently reproduced the surface of symbolic objects in places of historical significance like the Berlin Wall, also trees, thereby creating various textures on the surface of the objects. I have been honored with prestigious awards such as the *Herbert Hofmann Prize* 2022 and the *Robbe & Berking Award* 2019. A finalist for the *Loewe Craft Prize* in 2021, my works are held in numerous museums and collections worldwide.

@sunghocho417

Sarah Cossham

1979
lebt in München DE

1997–2000 Ausbildung zur Silberschmiedin, BFS Glas und Schmuck Kaufbeuren-Neugablonz (Nikolaus Epp)
2003 Gründung der Werkstatt-Galerie tragbar in München
2022 Gründung des Podcasts *others & me. Der Podcast für Zeitgenössischen Schmuck und Gerät*
2023 Gaststudium in der Klasse für Schmuck und Gerät, AdBK in München (Prof. Karen Pontoppidan)

Auszeichnungen
2019 *Ebbe Weiss-Weingart Silberpreis, 19. Silbertriennale International*

Andreas Decker

1958
lebt in Diekholzen DE

1978–1981 Ausbildung zum Goldschmied
1982–1986 Studium Produkt-/Metallgestaltung
1999–2002 Lehrauftrag, FH Hildesheim
seit 2000 Lehrauftrag, Staatliche Zeichenakademie Hanau
seit 2011 Leiter der Silberschmiedeklasse, Staatliche Zeichenakademie Hanau
2018 Veranstalter des 18. internationalen Silberschmiedeforums in Hanau

Auszeichnungen
1991 Hauptpreis des internationalen Wettbewerbes *Metall und Licht*
1997 *Niedersächsischer Förderpreis*
1998 *Hessischer Staatspreis*
2007 2. Preis Hauptwettbewerb, *15. Silbertriennale International*
2012 3. Preis *Silver Moves* des internationalen Silberschmiedeforums

Arbeiten in öffentlichen Sammlungen
- Zucker-Museum, Berlin
- Museum für Kunst und Gewerbe Hamburg
- Deutsches Goldschmiedehaus Hanau
- Marienkirche, Hanau
- Handwerkskammer Koblenz
- Die Neue Sammlung – The Design Museum, München
- Musée Mandet, Riom
- Collection Vic Janssens, DIVA Museum for Diamonds, Jewellery and Silver, Antwerpen

Hanyi Feng

1998
lives in Birmingham GB

Hanyi Feng is a jewellery and object maker from China. She completed her BA and MA in 2023 at the School of Jewellery, Birmingham. Texture and surface application are always the key elements of expression in her practice, fusing and formalising different textures is the way she captures the flowing moment and status. They stimulate the sense of sight and tactile for both the maker and the audience, enriching the language of the work. Her current work explores different perspectives on the structure of drinking vessels, disassembling and assembling the traditional forms. The group drinking vessel set captures the circumstances of group activities, emphasis on sharing, toasting and ritualistic pleasure of drinking. Hanyi's work also aims to redirect the focus to the objects themselves and also brings ritualistic action to modern life.

@hyf_workingspace

Gretal Ferguson

1982
lives in Adelaide AU

Gretal Ferguson creates conceptual exhibition work using traditional craft skills in a sculptural setting, challenging the utilitarian traditions of her craft while honouring what came before. With the material process an integral part of her conceptual motivation, Ferguson embraces the arduous nature of silversmithing, using the hours of hammering to explore the work both aesthetically and conceptually, allowing it to unfold in a way it wouldn't if the process was quick and less laborious.

@gretalferguson
www.gretalferguson.com

Benedikt Förster-Heyne

1967
lebt in Aachen DE

1986–1990 Ausbildung zum Goldschmied, Goldschmiede Spölgen, Tübingen
1992–1996 Mitarbeit als Geselle im elterlichen Betrieb
1992–1995 berufsbegleitender Besuch der Handwerksakademie Gut Rosenberg, Aachen-Horbach
1995 Abschlussprüfung zum Gestalter im Handwerk
1996 Meisterprüfung, Meisterdesigner
1996–2000 Mitarbeit als Meister im elterlichen Betrieb
2000–2015 Mitinhaber der GOLD + SILBERSCHMIEDE FÖRSTER
seit 2016 Alleininhaber der GOLD + SILBERSCHMIEDE FÖRSTER

Auszeichnungen
1996 *1. Preis Junges Handwerk NRW*

Ausstellungen
1997 Wettbewerb-Ausstellung *Camelot 1115* Krakau
1998 *12. Silbertriennale International*
2007 Maison des Métiers d'Art Lüttich
2009 *pur pur* Aachen
2010 *16. Silbertriennale International*
2013 *MANUFACTUM* Dortmund
2019 *MANUFACTUM* Museum für Angewandte Kunst, Köln
2022 *KUNSTWERKSTATT EUREGIO* Museum Zinkhütter Hof, Stolberg
2023 *MANUFACTUM* Museum für Angewandte Kunst, Köln

@goldschmiede.foerster
www.goldschmiede-foerster.de

Andreas Frank

1949
lebt in Neulingen-Bauschlott DE

1967–1972 Lehre als Goldschmied, Goldschmiedeschule Pforzheim und Kassel
1973–1977 FHG Pforzheim (Prof. Reinhold Reiling)
1975 Meisterprüfung im Goldschmiedehandwerk
1977 Diplom-Designer FH
1975–1976 Silberschmiede Sigurd Persson / Prof. K. Ullrich
1977–1980 Schmuckindustrie Pforzheim und Norwegen
1981–1988 eigene Werkstatt in Böblingen
1988–2015 Lehrer, Berufskolleg für Design, Schmuck und Gerät, Pforzheim
2015–2024 eigene Werkstatt in Neulingen-Bauschlott

Ausstellungen
2022 *20. Silbertriennale International*
2023 *OFFENE ATELIERS PFORZHEIM* Enzkreis Katharinentaler Hof Atelier Eckhard Bausch
2024 *PEACE-PIECES* Galerie Schmucke, Berlin
- Galerie Weinberger, Nürnberg
- *OFFENE ATELIERS PFORZHEIM* Enzkreis Katharinentaler Hof Atelier Eckhard Bausch
- *Lebenslöffel* Hammerclub Treffen, Museumshof Lehnsahn

www.andreasfrankbk.de

Luise Fritzsche
1999
lebt in Bad Endorf DE

seit 2022 Ausbildung zur Silberschmiedin, BFS Glas und Schmuck Kaufbeuren-Neugablonz

Kristóf András Gelley
1983
lebt in Budajenő HU

Ich bin ein ungarischer Silberschmied und Metalldesigner im Alter von 41 Jahren. Seit 20 Jahren bin ich in der Silberschmiedekunst und seit 14 Jahren in der Metallgestaltung tätig. Ich interessiere mich für Silberobjekte, die besonders und nützlich sind. Einfaches, praktisches Design, klare Ideen und handwerkliches Können. Ich suche Formen, die neu sind, sich aber anfühlen, als hätte es sie schon immer gegeben.

Als Spross der Familie Giergl stamme ich aus einer Tiroler Künstler- und Handwerkerfamilie, die seit 300 Jahren Kultur und Handwerk in Budapest betreibt. Ich habe an der Moholy-Nagy Universität für Kunst und Design und ein Semester an der HAWK in Hildesheim studiert.

Seit meinem Diplom im Jahr 2010 arbeite ich in meinem Unternehmen und fertige Objekte für den Sakral- und Innenraum sowie Pokale und Gefäße. Zurzeit beschäftige ich mich mit der Zukunft von Silberobjekten.

www.gmmuvek.com

Kirsten Haydon
1973
lives in Melbourne AU

Kirsten Haydon investigates the potential of gold and silversmithing to communicate human experience and connections with the environment. Kirsten completed a PhD in 2009 and has been teaching at the School of Fine Art, RMIT University in Melbourne since 2002. Kirsten travelled to Antarctica as a New Zealand Antarctic Arts Fellow in 2004. Her art practice crafts and explores connections and observations of the environment through concepts of historic photography and micromosaics. Site and archival studies inform works which aim to engage the act of remembering and the fragile futures of ice by assembling and drawing on metal and enamel surfaces.

@kirstenhaydon

Jiahn Hong
1993
lives in Seoul KR

Jiahn Hong is a metalsmith artist based in South Korea. She holds an MFA from Kookmin University and a BFA from Konkuk University. Her work explores the intersection of geometry, materiality and form, emphasizing the harmonious balance of structure and fluidity. In 2024, she held her first solo exhibition, *Exploring Vessel*, at Gallery WANNMUL in Seoul, and has participated in numerous group exhibitions, including *The Geography of Objects* (2023) and *Past and Present* (2024). She received an Honorable Mention at the 2023 *Cheongju International Craft Competition*.

@hhon9

Marian Hosking
1948
lives in Rye AU

Marian Hosking is an educator, jeweller and silversmith. With the benefit of intensive practice she has developed a personal vocabulary in her work to express a specific vision and interpretation of the qualities of Australian light and landscape in the detail of botanical specimens. She uses the drill and jeweller's saw together with lost wax castings and favours the soft white sheen of silver, with its evasive highlights and shifting shadows.

She has held 16 solo exhibitions in Australia. She is represented in Australia by Funaki, Melbourne and Bilk, Canberra. She has been an educator in her field for over thirty years, including at Monash University. She received her PhD in 2009, Monash University, an MA and Diploma of Art-Gold and Silversmithing in 1970 from RMIT. She is committed to the promotion of and dialogue around contemporary jewellery and contemporary art practice.

@hoskingmarian

Iris Hummer
1983
lives in Vienna AT

Iris Hummer is an Austrian artist who focuses on themes such as movement, transformation and the traces that these processes leave behind. Jewellery is used as a performative medium that enables viewers to have interactive experiences. She develops objects that function as tools to expand the scope of action and invite the viewer to reflect on their own experiences, memories and values. She is fascinated by processes and ambiguities that she wants to make visible in order to explore why things are the way they are. Her artistic inspiration stems from her childhood, influenced by her family's artistic background, especially street theatre and painting. These experiences taught her to allow spontaneity and to react to the unexpected. Her engagement with the object is always an investigation, an experiment and an exploration. Openness, curiosity and a playful approach characterise her artistic work.

She trained in Vienna at the University of Applied Arts and at the ar.co in Lisbon. Since October 2021 she is in the Master's programme of Fine Arts and Jewellery in Idar-Oberstein. She will complete her Master's degree in Idar-Oberstein at the end of 2024.

@i.hummer_

David Huycke

1967
lives in Sint-Niklaas BE

David Huycke is a visual artist and researcher who explores a variety of media, but is best known for his innovative approach to metalwork, more specifically the use of granulation in larger sculptural silver objects.

Huycke graduated in 1989 from Sint Lucas Antwerp. In 2010 he earned his PhD in Arts from the KU Leuven and Hasselt University with the project *The Metamorphic Ornament: Re-Thinking Granulation*, a practice-based research on the contemporary artistic relevance of the ancient technique of granulation. David Huycke is now professor at the PXL-MAD School of Arts Hasselt and at the Faculty of Architecture and Arts at Hasselt University.

Huycke's artistic work balances on the edge of figuration and abstraction. He draws inspiration from cosmic themes, such as planets and atoms, clouds, night and day, as well as from concepts such as darkness, horizon, order and chaos. His aim is to convey the poetic essence of these enigmatic phenomena through the medium of silver.

His silver objects are included in numerous public collections worldwide. Furthermore, Huycke's work has been recognized with several awards, including the *Bayerischer Staatspreis* in both 2007 and 2019, as well as the *Robbe & Berking Preis* at the *20th Silver Triennial International* in 2022.

@david.huycke
www.davidhuycke.com

Inhwan Jeon

1991
lives in Daegu KR

Inhwan Jeon is a contemporary Korean craft artist who works with objects, sculpture, and installation art. He holds a Bachelor's (2016) and Master's degree (2018) in Metal Art and Design from Seoul National University of Science and Technology. In 2024, he completed his Master of Fine Arts degree in the Metals and Jewelry program at the Rochester Institute of Technology in New York.

Inhwan Jeon was awarded the *Grand Prize* at the *20th Iksan Korean Craft Exhibition* in 2019 and was selected for the Society of North American Goldsmiths' juried exhibitions in 2022 and 2023. He has gained recognition for his thought-provoking work.

His practice explores the intersection of profound human emotions, existence, and cultural narratives, with metal as his primary medium. Recently, Jeon has focused on the study of human superstitions and taboos, developing these themes through sculptural works and objects. He draws inspiration from the worn surfaces of sculptures and statues in human society, which bear the traces of repeated human touch, as well as the visual language of stone towers – symbols of human aspiration that evoke a sense of taboo.

@jeoninhwan

Yong-il Jeon

1956
lives in Seoul KR

1979 BFA Seoul National University, Seoul
1989 MFA Miami University, Ohio
1990–2021 Professor, Dept. of Metalwork and Jewelry, Kookmin University

Exhibitions
2013 *Mit der Zeit gehen* Galerie Rosemarie Jäger, Hocheim
2015 *Korea Now* Musée des Arts Décoratifs, Paris
2017 *Koreanisch – Kunsthandwerk aus Korea* Bayerischer Kunstgewerbeverein, Munich
2017 *Tresor Contemporary Craft* Messe Schweiz, Basel
2018 *Da-Kyung* Tea Culture exhibition, Tokyo University of the Arts Gallery
2018 Internationale Handwerksmesse, Munich

Awards
1991 *The Prize of Korean Craft Council*
1993 *Dong-A Craft Award, The 21th Dong-A National Crafts Competition*
1995 *Silver Prize, Miyagi International Design Competition*
2018 *Bayerischer Staatspreis*

Public Collections
• Victoria and Albert Museum, London
• Die Neue Sammlung – The Design Museum, Munich
• Seoul Museum of Craft Art
• National Museum of Modern and Contemporary Art Korea, Seoul
• Chiwoo Craft Museum, Seoul

@yong1jeon
www.yongiljeon.kr

Jae Hui Jeong

1992
lives in Seoul KR

Jae Hui Jeong received her BFA for Jewelry Arts and Design from Wonkwang University in 2015, and her MFA in Metalwork and Jewelry from Kookmin University in 2021. Currently, she is energetically performing as a metal craft artist and teaches metal hammering techniques to students at Wonkwang University and Dankook University. She has participated in numerous group exhibitions and held her first solo exhibition, *IN AND OUT*, at Choeunsook Gallery in 2024, showing variable works.

Her works are based on hammering techniques on sheet metals, which brings curiosity for hidden forms and spaces under the hollow metal surfaces. She focuses on the boundaries between internal and external spaces and tries to capture the dynamic energy from them. She experiments and practices to uncover the beauty with the hard materiality of metal objects.

Awards
2020 Honorable Mention, *Iksan Korea Craft Competition*
2021 Honorable Mention, *Iksan Korea Craft Competition*
• Excellence Award, *Craft Trend Fair* Korea
• Special Prize, *Cheongju International Craft Competition*
2022 4th Prize in Youth Promotion, *20th Silver Triennial International*
2023 Honorable Mention, *Iksan Korea Craft Competition*
• Honorable Mention, *Cheongju International Craft Competition*

@jjhuii_

Carl Kankowsky

1998
lebt in München DE

2020–2024 Ausbildung zum Silberschmied, Staatliche Zeichenakademie Hanau
seit 2024 Studium in der Klasse für Schmuck und Gerät, AdBK in München (Prof. Karen Pontoppidan)

Auszeichnungen
2023 1. Preis der Gestaltung der *Silbernen Halbkugel* des Deutschen Nationalkomitees für Denkmalschutz
2024 Celia Holtzer Stipendium, Gesellschaft für Goldschmiedekunst e.V.

Ausstellungen
2022 *20. Silbertriennale International*

@carlmkankowsky

Sang Hoon Kim

1986
lives in Yongin KR

Craft is the act of accumulating as one moves the body into the outcome. Regardless of the outcome, by building the time, it is born into a shape. Hammering to create a shape is thought to be a way to show these time-building characteristics. The encounter between metal and hammering resembles the narrative that forms the meeting of people. Depending on how the correlation of materials and hands, the hammer and the anvil is dealt with, we see different responses, noticing that the impression of the first encounter is not the same. Namely, the mastery of the tools and the hands will lead to a conclusion culminating in a genuine relationship that encompasses all moments.

Meanwhile, our five senses and memories are open to the world. We constantly sense and perceive, but we are not aware of all that. Experiences are recognized through the five senses and imprinted. I remember the experiences in the emotions using the metal technique and then layer them in the material. The routines or anecdotes are not special. It may be the inspiration of a beer with my wife after work (*Routine Vase*) or it may be the touch of the skin and the shaking of the hair that the mountain breeze cools the body (*Anecdote Vase*). These are everyday or memorable senses that we can all experience.

Through this accumulation of time, my work does not end with self-comfort. It is an opportunity to remind us of each experience and sense. It can be taking time off, some consolation, or a small echo in the mind.

Catherine Large

1964
lives in Brisbane AU

Catherine Large is a contemporary jeweller and metalsmith, her practice encompasses silversmithing and vitreous enamelling. Catherine has a Bachelor of Visual Art from Sydney College of the Arts, and a Masters of Visual Art from Queensland College of Art, Griffith University.

She combines her studio practice with teaching in university settings and adult education. Catherine has been making original jewellery, objects and flatware in precious metal for over 35 years. She often works with recycled and reused materials, both precious and non-precious, in a studio that is an efficient but compact space. She draws on her experiences of her environment, travel, and the nature of »stuff« to inform her work, which is a contemplative process of considering materials, taking time to think about the creation of objects and using her hands and tools to bring the ideas to fruition. She remains particularly interested in objects and flatware, a focus of her original training. She sees making as an opportunity to communicate ideas and to engage in notions such as sustainability and quality in craftsmanship.

Catherine has been the recipient of a number of grants and has held solo exhibitions as well as participating regularly in group exhibitions both nationally and internationally. Her work is held in both public and private collections.

@catherinelarge_jeweller
www.catherinelarge.com

Annette Lechler

1961
lebt in Karlsruhe DE

1982–1986 Studium Bildhauerei, Freiburg
1989–1994 Studium Schmuck und Gerät HFG Pforzheim, DAAD Niederlande
1997–1998 Lehrtätigkeit Gestaltung FH Trier/Idar-Oberstein
Seit 2000 wird ihr der persönliche Austausch mit Menschen, die Interesse an den wandelbaren Zwischenspielen finden, sowie die Zeit zum Entwickeln immer wichtiger.

Auszeichnungen
1998 *Staatspreis Baden-Württemberg*, Anerkennung
1999 *Hessischer Staatspreis*
2010 *Best of Germany Exhibit Prize* Philadelphia Museum of Art, US
2017 1. Preis Zeughausmesse Berlin
2022 *Staatspreis Baden-Württemberg*

Ausstellungen
2018–2024 MK&G Messe Hamburg
2019 *19. Silbertriennale International*
2021 *Kunsthandwerk ist Kaktus. Die Sammlung von 1945 bis heute* Museum Angewandte Kunst, Frankfurt am Main
2022 *20. Silbertriennale International*

www.lechler.biz

Zhizhong Li

1991
lives in Hangzhou CN

After graduating from the Decorative Arts and Design program at the China Academy of Art in 2015, I officially joined the studio of renowned Chinese jewelry artist Ni Xianou, beginning an eight-year career as an artist assistant. During this period, I learned immensely and grew tremendously. Working in a professional art studio allowed me to understand the latest trends and refine my craftsmanship in cutting-edge art jewelry. This experience was the best nourishment for deepening my understanding of contemporary jewelry.

Driven by personal growth and a passion for metalsmithing, in 2020 I re-entered the China Academy of Art to pursue graduate studies, further focusing on contemporary art jewelry and artisanal metal vessels. I graduated in 2024 with a master's degree. This journey has allowed me to delve deeper into the world of avant-garde jewelry and decorative metalwork.

Bo-Ting Lin

2000
lives in Tainan TW

2019 Dept. of Spatial Design of Kun Shan University in Taiwan
2021 Basic silversmithing, Yuan Silver Gallery
2022 Advanced silversmithing, Yuan Silver Gallery
2023 Silversmithing studies, Bergin studio

Qiwei Liu

1993
lives in Edinburgh GB

This project draws inspiration from the concept of the cairn, a traditional stone marker symbolizing memory. Throughout history, humans have employed various rituals to honor the deceased, it fuels my creative practice. Through craft, I confront the chaos of conflict, disaster, and renewal, exploring symbols of death, rebirth, and memory that continuously collide in modern society.

In this series, I use ashes as the primary medium. I blend bone ashes with enamel, firing them at high temperatures to create textured, stone-like sculptures. Bone ashes with enamel powder are blended, giving rise to a novel enamel variant. In contrast to traditional enamel with metal base, this technique creates an independent three-dimensional enamel form. Through fire, the bone-enamel mixture expands to form a foam-like internal structure, resulting in a light weight with textured resemblance to rough stones on the surface. Efcolor enamel encases the bone-enamel in a wearable silver »cupcake case«, for aesthetic enhancement, complemented by the application of gold foil.

In this process, the ashes and enamel elevate each other – not only as a physical transformation but also as a reshaping of emotions and culture. The process of making is like an ancient ritual – the end of life becoming the beginning of rebirth. The candlestick and incense holder transcend their functional roles, embodying a primal sense of ritual and a connection to memory. It feels like an end, but also a beginning.

@qiwei.liu_jeweller
www.liuqiwei.co.uk

Christine Matthias

1969
lebt in Halle (Saale) DE

1992–1996 Studium Innenarchitektur, Hochschule Hannover
1995 Gastsemester am Politecnico di Milano
1996–2002 Studium im Schmuck, Burg Giebichenstein Kunsthochschule Halle (Saale) (Dorothea Prühl)
seit 2002 freischaffend in Halle (Saale)
2019 Lehrauftrag Schmuck/Metallgestaltung, HAWK in Hildesheim

Auszeichnungen
2002 3. Preis Nachwuchsförderwettbewerb *Schmuck und Gerät*, Hanau
2008 Marzee Prize Galerie Marzee, Nijmegen
2015 *Grassipreis* der Sparkasse Leipzig
2017 Arbeitsstipendium, Kunststiftung Sachsen-Anhalt
• Kloster Bergesche Stiftung
• Artist in Residence, Jakob Bengel-Stiftung, Idar-Oberstein

Ausstellungen
2022 Galerie Marzee, Nijmegen
• *SCHMUCK + IMAGE* Grassi Museum, Leipzig
• *Meister der Moderne* Galerie Handwerk, München
2023 Friedrich Becker Preis Düsseldorf Hanau
• *Ausformungen* Galerie Schmucke, Berlin
• MK&G Messe, Museum für Kunst und Gewerbe Hamburg
2024 *Wir sind Kunst. 20 Jahre Kunststiftung Sachsen-Anhalt* Halle (Saale)
• *Das Ereignis* Kunstverein Wiligrad, Lübstorf
• *Schmuck Portraits* Galerie Slavik, Wien
• *Grassimesse*, Leipzig

Arbeiten in öffentlichen Sammlungen
• CODA Museum, Apeldoorn
• Museum Bückeburg
• Dallas Museum of Art
• Kunstmuseum Moritzburg Halle (Saale), Kulturstiftung Sachsen-Anhalt
• Jakob Bengel-Stiftung, Idar-Oberstein
• Grassi Museum, Leipzig
• The Marzee Collection, Galerie Marzee, Nijmegen
• Universität Rostock

@christine.matthias.jewellery
www.christinematthias.de

Militsa Milenkova

1995
lives in Glasgow GB

Militsa Milenkova is a Bulgarian artist, designer and maker. She grew up in Greece and was introduced to metal working in 2017 as an intern for a contemporary jeweller. After that, she moved to Scotland where she acquired an HND in Jewellery Making from the City of Glasgow College and later graduated with a first-class BA (Hons) in Silversmithing and Jewellery from the Glasgow School of Art. During her studies, she has gained further experience working as a jeweller in a professional environment as well as spending a month as artist in residence at Plattform Schmuckkunst.

She creates functional, decorative and wearable objects as a means of communicating her thoughts and feelings and draws inspiration mainly from her surroundings and personal experiences. In her practice she explores various concepts that intrigue her, while triggering her creativity by experimenting with different materials. Through the use of pre-existing ordinary objects, she challenges the notion of value and poses the question of what is considered precious and why.

@militsa_milenkova
www.militsamilenkova.com

Alex O'Connor

1969
lives in St Just GB

I came to silver from a background in Fine Art and Sculpture. Accordingly, my silverware merges an inherent understanding of form, composition, balance and surface with the specific disciplines of contemporary craft.

Collections are created through a process that begins with walking through the landscape and moves into drawing and model making. The resulting pieces, often vessel forms, bring together ideas of both external and internal landscape. These objects are essential, in that they use only what is needed to convey meaning.

The world is a beautiful place, filled with wonders, but also cacophonous, baffling, chaotic and overwhelming at times. I convert these sensations into silverware and wearable sculptures that are suffused with harmony, composure, poise and serenity.

@movingmetal
www.alexoconnorsilver.co.uk

Byungik Park

1993
lives in Tokyo JP

2012–2018 Metal Craft, BFA Musashino Art University
2018–2020 Metal Craft, MFA Musashino Art University
since 2020 Metal Craft, Research Assistant of Musashino Art University

Exhibitions
2018 *Musashino Art University Graduation Works 2017* Spiral Garden of Tokyo
• *Seikado The Ima-kara Mame-sara Metalworks Exhibition* Seikado, Kyoto
2019 *19th Silver Triennial International*
2020 *Musashino Art University Graduation Works 2019* Spiral Garden of Tokyo
2021 *Cheongju International Craft Biennale* Cheongju
2022 *20th Silber Triennial International*
2023 *Inhorgenta* Munich

Snow falling from sky feels like magic, covering the world and creating a special moment. I also imagined the snow piling up on the ground as a moment where heaven and earth come together as one. I captured that moment through an object representing a pillar that connects heaven and earth.

@p_byungik

Jieun Park

1980
lives in Seoul KR

Jieun Park received her MFA and BFA in Metal Craft from Konkuk University and her PhD in Metal Craft from Kookmin University. She operates her own studio and works as a craft artist. Since 2011, she has been teaching metal craft, jewelry, and history of jewelry design at university. She has participated in over 100 group exhibitions, including six solo exhibitions. In 2017, she participated in a workshop at the Victoria and Albert Museum in London. In 2019, she won *TOP11* at the *Cheongju International Craft Biennale*, the *Metal Craftsman of the Year Award* in Korea, and the Professional category award at Spain's *Enjoia't Awards*. Her works have been collected by prestigious institutions such as the Victoria and Albert Museum and the Seoul Museum of Craft Art.

She has been dedicated to studying how to create large shapes by repetitively combining small pieces. Through years of working with repetitive structures and circulation, she has contemplated the mental world it evokes, experiencing the process of healing within the continuous labor. Since 2019, she has been expanding her artistic spectrum to include objects and installation works.

Wu Peng

1991
lives in Hangzhou CN

The fusion of pebbles and artifacts is a projection and reflection of time. Over millions of years, nature has sculpted pebbles into their current form, while our ancestors, through wisdom and craftsmanship, transformed various materials into practical vessels. These artifacts not only carry the historical context and cultural essence of their makers but also convey a sense of life's vitality. When pebbles meet artifacts, they seem to narrate their own stories, allowing us to more deeply feel the passage of time and the rhythm of life. I often imagine how our ancestors made the first container. The vessels of the Neolithic Age exude a powerful sense of life. These artifacts, carrying the era of their creators, are presented before us. In the moment of their completion, it seems as if they have found a way to preserve time. Human will and spirit are captured within the artifacts, as if they have obtained a true model of time. Time is intricately carved into these objects for the long term. This series of works is crafted from Mokume-gane metal, a material that I have developed and produced myself. The shaping of the artifacts is achieved through the method of forging.

Christine Ramel

1962
lives in Stockholm SE

I have been a silversmith and goldsmith for over 35 years. I run my own workshop in Stockholm and create unique jewelry, hollowware and art objects.

I have my background in, among others, silver and goldsmithing, glassblowing and graphic design. I mix modern aesthetics with classic forging.

I began my craft journey at Stockholm's Art School, followed by pattern construction, design at Stockholm's Tailor Academy and studies in painting and sculpture. My interest in materials led me to Orrefors Glass School and on to silversmithing and goldsmithing. Under masters like Karl-Heinz Sauer, I deepened my knowledge of hollowware eight years ago.

I have exhibited works both internationally and nationally, most recently at the Tokyo Metropolitan Art Museum (2024) and the *20th Silver Triennial International*. In Sweden, my art has been shown in several museums and galleries. Right now I'm exhibiting at Liljevalchs, Stockholm and Galleri Montan, Copenhagen.

My work combines sculptural elements with graphic simplicity and function. Since 2018, I have been part of Nutida Svenskt Silver, which represents Swedish contemporary silversmiths.

Callum Partridge

1995
lives in Stroud GB

Callum Partridge was born in Stroud, Gloucestershire, England. During his formative years he was drawn to a community workshop where he first discovered his love of metalwork and silversmithing. It was here that at the age of 13, that he made his first piece of jewellery and went on to study Jewellery and Silversmithing at London Metropolitan University. Following a residency of two years, Callum returned to Stroud in 2020 to set up his own workshop.

@c.m.partridge

Christoph Pilsel

1991
lebt in Hanau DE

Im Februar 2016 schloss ich meine Ausbildung zum Silberschmied erfolgreich ab und erweiterte mein Wissen durch weitere Semester an der Staatlichen Zeichenakademie Hanau. Als freier Schmuckdesigner und Schmuckfotograf konnte ich wertvolle Berufserfahrung sammeln. Von 2022 bis 2024 besuchte ich die Fachschule der Staatlichen Zeichenakademie Hanau, um den Gold- und Silberschmiedemeister sowie den Gestalter im Handwerk zu erlangen. Derzeit bin ich als pädagogischer Mitarbeiter und Ausbilder für Metall in einem Bildungswerk tätig.

@christoph.pilsel

Yeunhee Ryu

1962
lives in Seoul KR

Born in 1962 in Yeongeon-dong, Seoul, I grew up surrounded by the charm of traditional Korean architecture and the lively atmosphere of Changgyeonggung Palace. My early memories of exploring the palace's gardens and zoo greatly influenced my appreciation for cultural aesthetics. After studying crafts at university, I delved into the intricate patterns of palatial designs, which later became a foundational aspect of my work.

Throughout my career, I have specialized in metal crafts, focusing on creating functional tableware and objects. My recent projects include designing teapots, cups, and brewing sets, all crafted to enhance everyday experiences. I strive to blend natural forms with practical use, aiming to express warmth and comfort in my creations. My work reflects a deep connection to Korean culture, merging traditional aesthetics with contemporary functionality. I am dedicated to exploring the details of my craft, ensuring that each piece resonates with both beauty and usability. My journey as an artist continues to be driven by a passion for cultural heritage and a desire to share that through my work.

@smithryu

Helena Schepens

1981
lives in Antwerp BE

Helena Schepens studied Silversmithing at the Royal Academy of Fine Arts Antwerp (2000–2004) and at the RCA London (2004–2006). Since 2007 she runs her own workshop in Antwerp. Also in 2007, Helena received the *Sterckshof Commission* for the silver museum Sterckshof in Antwerp.

Helena won the *Rotary International Award for Silversmithing* (2004), the *Goldsmith's Company Award for Silversmithing* (2006) and *The New Designers Award* (2006). She became finalist in the *Loewe Craft Prize* 2017 and was invited as a jury member in the 2018 edition. Also in 2018, Helena's work was included in the *Best of Europe* exhibition at *Homo Faber* in Venice. For the 3rd edition in 2024, *The Journey of Life*, she was invited again to contribute in the exhibition *Celebration*. Her work has been shown in various exhibitions in Europe, Russia, Japan and the USA.

She was selected for the *15th, 17th, 19th* and *20th Silver Triennial International*, and for the *European Prize of Applied Arts* (*BeCraft*) in 2015, 2019 and 2024.

Helena designed and made the *Henry van de Velde Awards* (2009–2013) and a reliquary for the Abbey van Park in Heverlee (2021). Princess Léa of Belgium visited Helena's studio in 2021 and included her work in the book *Métiers d'art* on art and craftsmanship. In 2023 her work was selected by WCCE to present Europe at the international art fair *Salon Révélations*, Grand Palais Éphémère in Paris.

@helenaschepens_metalwork
www.helenaschepens.com

Juliane Schölß

1977
lebt in Nürnberg DE

1996–1999 Ausbildung zur Silberschmiedin, BFS Glas und Schmuck Kaufbeuren-Neugablonz
1999–2000 Studium Kunstgeschichte und Romanistik, Universität Regensburg
2000–2004 Gesellenjahre als Silberschmiedin
2004 Meisterprüfung
2004–2010 Studium in der Klasse für Gold- und Silberschmieden, AdBK in Nürnberg (Prof. Ulla Mayer)
2009 Ernennung zur Meisterschülerin
seit 2010 eigenes Atelier in Nürnberg

Auszeichnungen
2005 Dritter Preis für Nachwuchskünstler Bezirk Oberbayern, München
2006 *BKV-Preis für Junges Kunsthandwerk* Bayerischer Kunstgewerbeverein, München
2011 *Danner Preis* München
2012 *Bayerischer Staatspreis*
• Nominiert für den *Justus Brinckmann Förderpreis*
2015 Nominiert für den *German Design Award – Newcomer* Frankfurt am Main
2019 *Ebbe Weiss-Weingart Preis*, 19. Silbertriennale International
2023 Zweiter Preis der Sonderausstellung *Zum Fest* Kunstverein Rosenheim
2024 Kunstpreis der Evangelischen Landeskirche Bayern, München

Arbeiten in öffentlichen Sammlungen
• Stadtmuseum, Ingolstadt
• Kolumba, Kunstmuseum des Erzbistum Köln
• Victoria and Albert Museum, London
• Danner-Stiftung, München

www.julianeschoelss.de

Gerrit Schulze Raestrup

1994
lebt in Hildesheim DE

2017–2021 Ausbildungsberuf zum Metallbauer Fachrichtung Metallgestaltung in der Schmiede Neuhammer bei Albrecht Morgenstern
2021 Geselle in der Schmiede Neuhammer in Olbernhau (Sachsen)
• eigene Werkstatt in Steinfurt
• Mitarbeit und Austausch mit verschiedenen spanischen Schmieden, unter anderem Friedrich Bramsteidel (Mazonovo) und Miquel Xirau (Vilanova del Vallès)
2022 Geselle in der Metallgestaltung und Kunstschlosserei Eickhoff, Havixbeck
seit 2022 Studium Metallgestaltung, HAWK in Hildesheim

@gerritschulzeraestrup

Regina Eva Sebold

1996
lebt in Heilsbronn DE

2012–2015 Ausbildung zur Holzbildhauerin, Berufsfachschule für Holzschnitzerei und Schreinerei, Berchtesgaden
2015–2017 Städtische Meisterschule für das Holzbildhauerhandwerk, München Abschluss mit dem Meisterbrief
2017–2020 Ausbildung zur Silberschmiedin, BFS Glas und Schmuck Kaufbeuren-Neugablonz
2020–2021 Ausbildung zur Goldschmiedin, BFS Glas und Schmuck Kaufbeuren-Neugablonz
seit 2021 Studium der Bildenden Kunst mit Schwerpunkt Schmuck und Gerät, AdBK in Nürnberg (Prof. Suska Mackert)

@ina.sebold

Yegyu Shin

1991
lives in Munich DE

I am currently studying Jewelry and Holloware at the AdBK in Munich, where I combine academic learning with my creative practice. In 2019, I studied Contemporary Sculpture at the same institution, exploring structural thinking, and since 2021, I have been developing my craft through silversmithing.
 My work focuses on exploring memory and personal narratives through silver hollowware and tableware. I reinterpret traditional forms from a contemporary perspective, aiming to blend craftsmanship with poetic storytelling. Most recently, I created a project titled *Toy of Time*, which reflects the flow of life and time through layered silver spoons.

Oliver Smith

1974
lives in Denman Prospect AU

Dr Oliver Smith began his tertiary studies in the Jewellery and Object Studio at Sydney College of the Arts, The University of Sydney and completed a Bachelor of Visual Arts in 1995. This was followed by a period of work experience, modelled on the traditional journeymanship, that saw him work for prominent silversmiths and metalworkers in Australia, New Zealand, Mexico, Germany, and England. Returning to formal study in the Gold and Silversmithing Workshop at the School of Art, The Australian National University in Canberra, Oliver gained First Class Honours in 2000, and a Master of Philosophy in 2003. Since that time Oliver has maintained an active research profile as an artist and has presented his work through exhibition nationally and internationally. From 2005 Oliver has worked as an academic at Sydney College of the Arts, The University of Sydney and in 2021 was awarded a Doctor of Philosophy.

Mariko Sumioka

1981
lives in Tokyo JP

Mariko Sumioka is a Japanese jeweller who spent her childhood in Brazil. She was always attracted by small and sparkling objects and also jewellery boxes. She studied Economics for her first degree followed by a job in the oil and gas upstream business. To seek her dream to be a jeweller, she left her job and completed her BA (Hons) in Jewellery and Silversmithing at Edinburgh College of Art, GB in 2011. While studying in Edinburgh, she developed her unique abstract aesthetic by combining precious metals with non-precious materials and her sculptural jewellery became her icon. In Sumioka's work, there are always small crafted details which viewers would discover and add their own stories. She set up her studio in London in 2012–2015 and returned to Tokyo in 2016. She exhibited her work internationally at art fairs and galleries.

@marikosumioka
www.marikosumioka.com

Lee Sungyeoul

1977
lives in Seoul KR

Lee Sungyeoul is a professor of metalwork at Kookmin University in South Korea, where he utilizes traditional silversmithing techniques and micro-welding technology. The contrast created by bringing together two similar yet opposite forms is a visual catharsis of the artist's everyday stories. In his work, the functional structure and tense, dignified form of a bottle are expressed with light straight lines and understated curves.

Mohammad Taghavi

1996
lebt in Hanau DE

Mein Name ist Mohammad Taghavi. Ich bin 28 Jahre alt, komme aus dem Iran und lebe seit 2016 in Deutschland. Seit 2019 absolviere ich meine Ausbildung an der Staatlichen Zeichenakademie Hanau, wo ich bald meine Zusatzausbildung zum Silberschmied abschließe. Das Handwerk der Gold- und Silberschmiedekunst ist für mich nicht nur ein Beruf, sondern eine Leidenschaft, die ich mit großer Freude verfolge. Dabei bin ich experimentierfreudig und stelle mich gerne neuen Herausforderungen, um mein handwerkliches Können und meine künstlerische Vision stetig weiterzuentwickeln.

Mein Stil zeichnet sich durch eine Vorliebe für massive, kantige Formen und klare Linien aus, die ich gezielt wähle, um eine markante, ausdrucksstarke Präsenz zu erzielen. In meiner Gestaltung lasse ich mich häufig von geometrischen Strukturen und architektonischen Formen inspirieren und setze diese Einflüsse in meinen Arbeiten um.

Jedes Werkstück – ob es eine skulpturale Wasserkaraffe oder ein außergewöhnliches Set aus Salz- und Pfefferstreuern ist – soll nicht nur funktional sein, sondern auch eine starke visuelle Präsenz und Individualität ausstrahlen.

@_vohuman_

Christoph Weißhaar

1980
lebt in Nürnberg DE

1998–2001 Ausbildung zum Silberschmied, BFS Glas und Schmuck Kaufbeuren-Neugablonz
2001 eigene Werkstatt in Landsberg am Lech
2004–2009 Studium in der Klasse für Gold- und Silberschmieden, AdBK in Nürnberg
2007–2008 Stipendium an der HfG Karlsruhe, Fachbereich Produktdesign
2009 Meisterschüler, AdBK in Nürnberg
seit 2009 eigenes Atelier in Nürnberg

2013–2014 Lehrtätigkeit, Staatliche Zeichenakademie Hanau
2016, 2018–2029 Lehrauftrag, AdBK in Nürnberg

Auszeichnungen
2002 Anerkennung Nachwuchsförderwettbewerb *Schmuck und Gerät*, Hanau
2013 1. Preis Nachwuchsförderwettbewerb, *17. Silbertriennale International*
2014 Anerkennung *Bayerischer Staatspreis* für Nachwuchsdesigner Bereich Gestaltendes Handwerk
2015 *Bayerischer Staatspreis*
2017 *Bayerischer Kunstförderpreis*, Spezialpreis *Schmuck und Gerät*
2018 *Hessischer Staatspreis*
2021 1. Preis *POTT:DESIGN-AWARD 2021* Deutsches Klingenmuseum, Solingen

Arbeiten in öffentlichen Sammlungen
• Museum Angewandte Kunst, Frankfurt am Main
• Kolumba, Kunstmuseum des Erzbistum Köln
• Victoria and Albert Museum, London

@chweisshaar
www.christoph-weisshaar.com

Tong Wu

1996
lives in Yinchuan CN

2016–2020 Undergraduate Degree, Xi'an Academy of Fine Arts
2021–2023 Postgraduate Degree in Jewellery and Metal, Royal College of Art

Awards
2022 *Contemporary Cutlery Design Competition*
2023 *Runner Up* United Kingdom Craft & Design Council Awards
• *Silversmiths – Silver Award* United Kingdom Craft Council of BC
2024 *Canada Inflow Contemporary Jewellery Exhibition and Conference* Hungary

@_tong_wu_
www.tongwujewellery.com

Siqiu Zhang

1996
lives in Hangzhou CN

Siqiu Zhang is a contemporary silversmith and art jewellery maker who graduated from the Birmingham School of Jewellery with a degree in Jewellery and Silversmithing in 2019. She furthered her postgraduate studies at the Edinburgh College of Art and is currently pursuing a second postgraduate degree at the China Academy of Art in the School of Crafts.

Siqiu has been recognized with several prestigious awards, including gold and silver prizes from the *Goldsmiths' Craft & Design Council* in Great Britain. Her artistic vision revolves around exploring the vitality of nature, using a metal language characterized by a delicate aesthetic. She is committed to discovering the inherent beauty of life within nature, exploring the intricate relationships between nature, life, and humanity. Her works are known for their finesse and elegance, employing the malleability of metal to convey the fragility and beauty of life, capturing the traces of nature and existence.

Siqiu Zhang continues to explore the intersection of traditional craftsmanship and contemporary art, pushing the boundaries of metal art to convey the subtle yet profound beauty of nature's organic forms.

@siqiu_zhang

Bildnachweis / Photo credits

516 studio 118, 119 · Farah Abdelhamid 60, 61 · Ole Akhøj 76, 77 · Apo studio 86, 87 · David Arzt 2–18, 20, 31, 36, 37, 42, 43, 48, 49, 54, 55, 197–207 · ATTO STUDIO Yong Jin Park 73 · Christoph Bauer 75 · Visuall Photography Michelle Bowden 125 · Tabea Helena Maki Brindöpke 81 · Ya Ping Cheng 83, 85 · S. Danielsson 149 · Andreas Decker 53, 57, 91–93 · Uwe Dettmar 34, 35, 38, 40, 52, 56, 62, 63, 66, 70–72, 74, 78–80, 82, 84, 90, 94–96, 98, 100–103, 106–109, 124, 126–127, 134, 135, 146, 148, 150, 151, 158, 159, 162–164, 168, 174, 175 · Knud Dobberke 68, 69 · Benedikt Förster-Heyne 99 · Luise Fritzsche 104, 105 · Alistair Fuller 114, 115 · Sangduk Han 166 · David Huycke 116, 117 · Hong 110, 111 · Shinichi Ichikawa 142, 143 · Yong-Il Jeon 39 · Eva Jünger 154, 155 · KC studio 86, 87 · Fred Kroh 112, 113 · Lighthouse Inc. 120–123 · Yo-Cheng Lin 132, 133 · Zhongquan Lin 130, 131 · Huaquin Liu 46, 47 · Tobias Mendoza 169 · Paul Mounsey 140, 141 · Munch Studio 50, 51 · Jieun Park 41 · Kwanghoon Park 167 · Connor Patterson 97 · Christoph Pilsel 147 · Ana Rodhila Prata 67 · Gerrit Schulze Raestrup 156, 157 · Matthias Ritzmann 136, 137 · Helena Schepens 152, 153 · Yegyu Shin 44, 45, 160, 161 · Julia Skupny 138, 139 · Yoon Chul Song 64, 65 · Mirei Takeuchi 88, 89 · Christoph Weißhaar 170, 171 · Peng Wu 144, 145 · Tong Wu 172, 173 · Ryo Yamashita 165

Umschlagabbildungen / Cover illustrations

vorne / front
Andreas Decker, *Roca*, 2024 (Detail), Seiten / Pages 92, 93
Foto / Photo: David Arzt

hinten / back
Sang Hoon Kim, *Routine Vase*, 2024 (Detail),
Seiten / Pages 122, 123
Foto / Photo: Lighthouse Inc.

innen vorne / inside front
Mariko Sumioka, *Roof and roof*, 2024 (Detail),
Seiten / Pages 164, 165
Foto / Photo: Uwe Dettmar

Jae Hui Jeong, *Conceal and Reveal*, 2024 (Detail),
Seiten / Pages 50, 51
Foto / Photo: Munch Studio

Ana Albuquerque, *restart*, 2023 (Detail), Seiten / Pages 66, 67
Foto / Photo: Uwe Dettmar

innen hinten / inside back
Militsa Milenkova & Callum Partridge, *Slow Down*, 2022 (Detail), Seiten / Pages 138, 139
Foto / Photo: Julia Skupny

Jae Hui Jeong, *Conceal and Reveal*, 2024 (Detail),
Seiten / Pages 50, 51
Foto / Photo: Munch Studio

Siqiu Zhang, *shimmering*, 2024 (Detail), Seiten / Pages 46, 47
Foto / Photo: Huaquin Liu

© 2025 arnoldsche
Art Publishers, Stuttgart,
und die Autoren / and the authors
© 2025 Gesellschaft für
Goldschmiedekunst e.V.

Alle Rechte vorbehalten. Vervielfältigung und Wiedergabe auf jegliche Weise (grafisch, elektronisch und fotomechanisch sowie der Gebrauch von Systemen zur Datenrückgewinnung), auch in Auszügen, nur mit schriftlicher Genehmigung der Copyright-Inhaber.
www.arnoldsche.com

All rights reserved. No part of this work may be reproduced or used in any forms or by any means (graphic, electronic or mechanical, including photocopying or information storage and retrieval systems) without the written permission from the copyright holders.
www.arnoldsche.com

Herausgeber / Editors
Malte Guttek,
Gesellschaft für
Goldschmiedekunst e.V.

Redaktion und Lektorat /
Editorial staff and editing
Tina Eberwein, Malte Guttek,
Julia Hohrein-Wilson, Tizia Puhane,
Ruth Schneider

Gestaltung / Design
Ina Bauer Studio, Stuttgart

Fotos Objektjury /
Photos Object Jury
David Arzt

Druck / Printed by
Offizin Scheufele Druck und
Medien GmbH & Co. KG

Buchbinder / Bound by
Idupa Schübelin GmbH

Bibliografische Informationen der
Deutschen Nationalbibliothek

Die Deutsche Nationalbibliothek verzeichnet diese Publikation in der der Deutschen Nationalbibliografie; detaillierte bibliografische Daten sind im Internet über www.dnb.de abrufbar.

Bibliographic information published by the Deutsche Nationalbibliothek

The Deutsche Nationalbibliothek lists this publication in the Deutsche Nationalbibliografie; detailed bibliographic data are available in the Internet at www.dnb.de

ISBN 978-3-89790-744-7
Made in Germany, 2025

Die vorliegende Publikation erscheint anlässlich der Ausstellung *21. Silbertriennale International 2025* im Deutschen Goldschmiedehaus Hanau, 30.03.–15.06.2025. Organisiert und konzipiert wird der weltweite Wettbewerb durch die Gesellschaft für Goldschmiedekunst e.V.

This present publication appears on the occasion of the exhibition *21st Silver Triennial 2025* at the Deutsches Goldschmiedehaus Hanau, 30.03.–15.06.2025. The worldwide competition is organized and conceived by the Gesellschaft für Goldschmiedekunst e.V.

Weitere Ausstellungen /
Forthcoming Exhibitions

DIVA, Museum voor Diamant, Juwelen en Zilver, Antwerpen (BE)
04.07.2025–30.09.2025

Schmuckmuseum Pforzheim (DE)
17.05.2026–17.01.2027

Die *21. Silbertriennale International 2025* entstand mit großzügiger Unterstützung von /
The *21st Silver Triennial 2025* has been realized with the generous support of

ROBBE & BERKING
— SILBER —

Hanau

ARTIMA
Die Kunstversicherung
der Mannheimer.

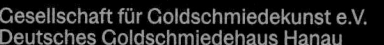

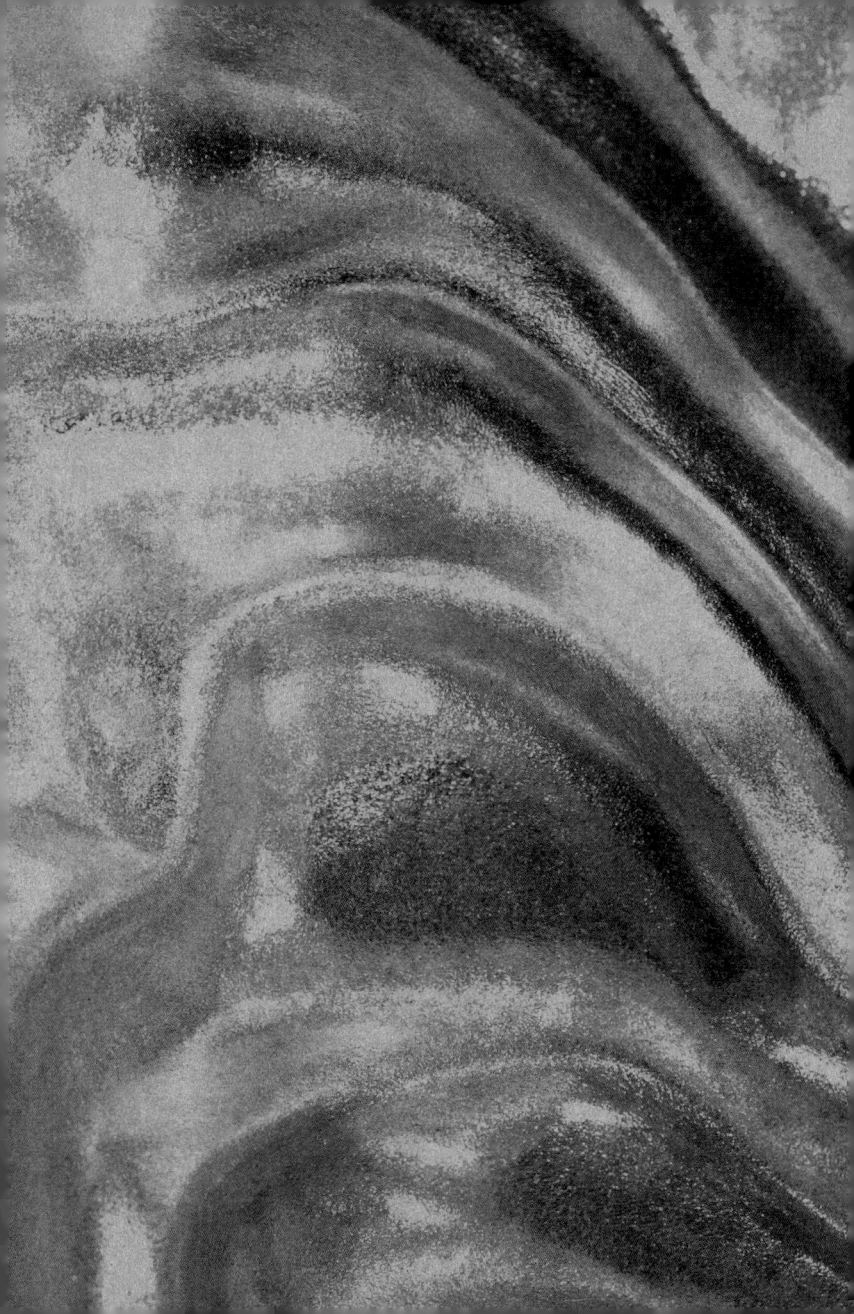

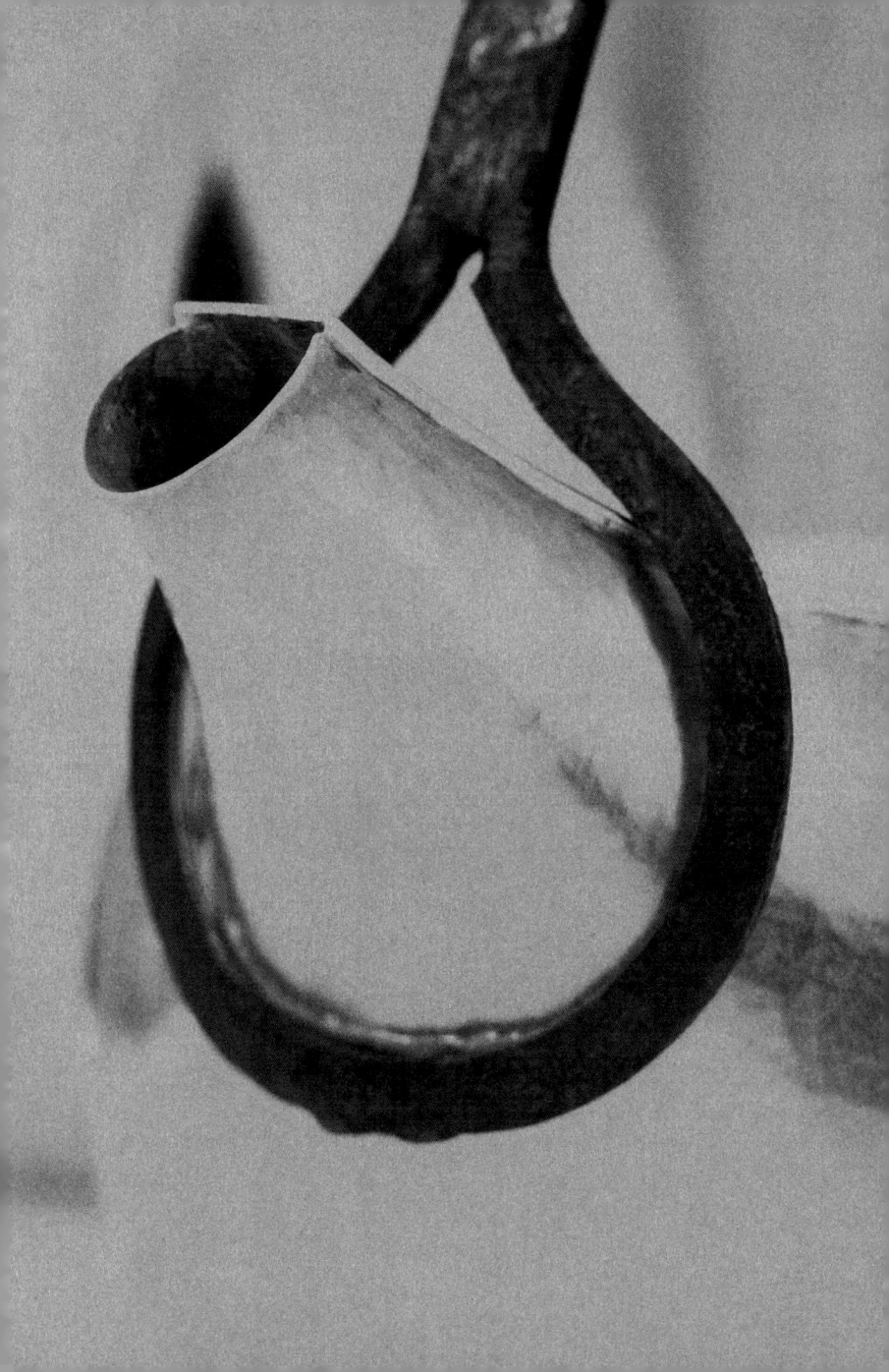

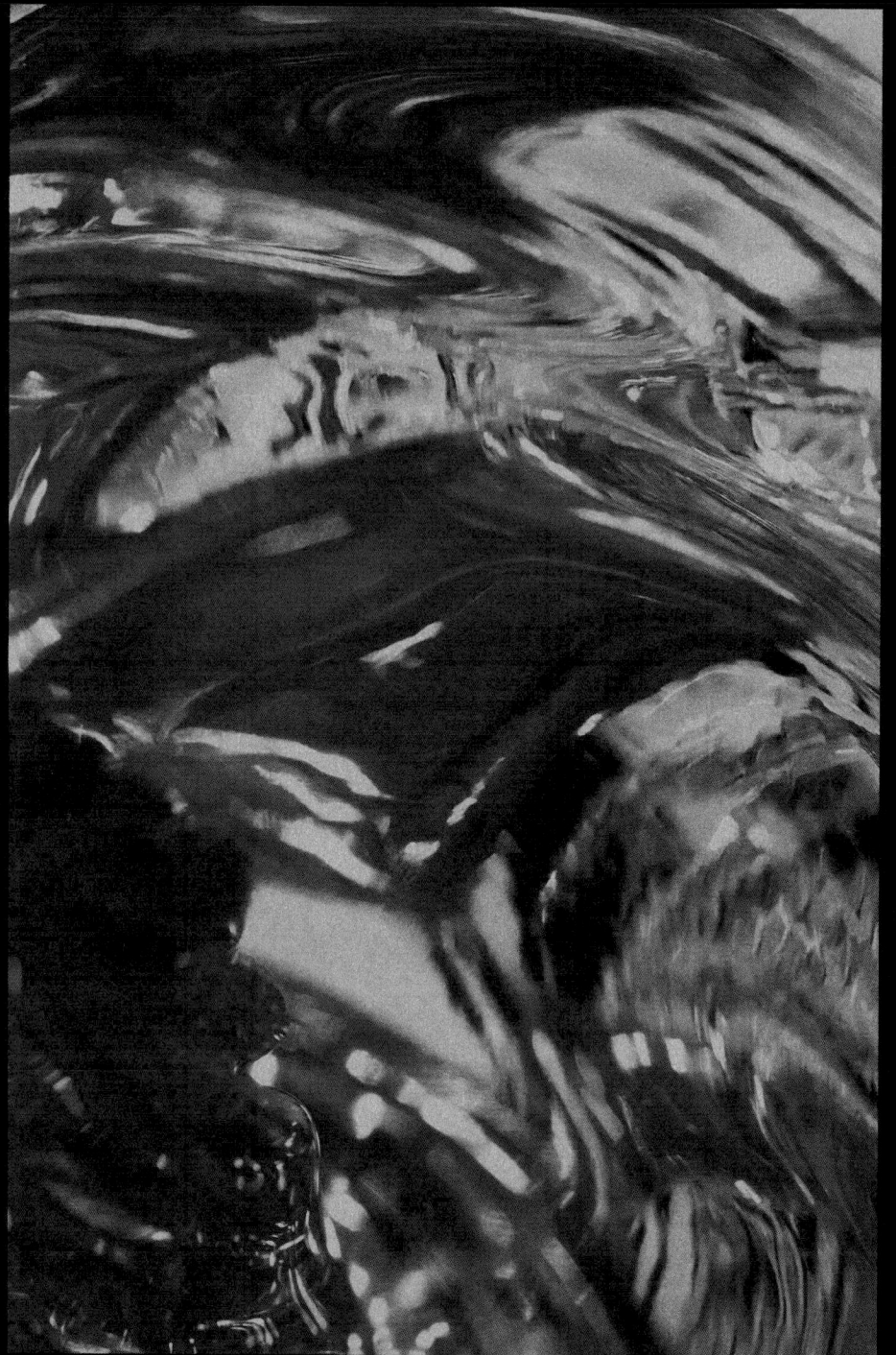

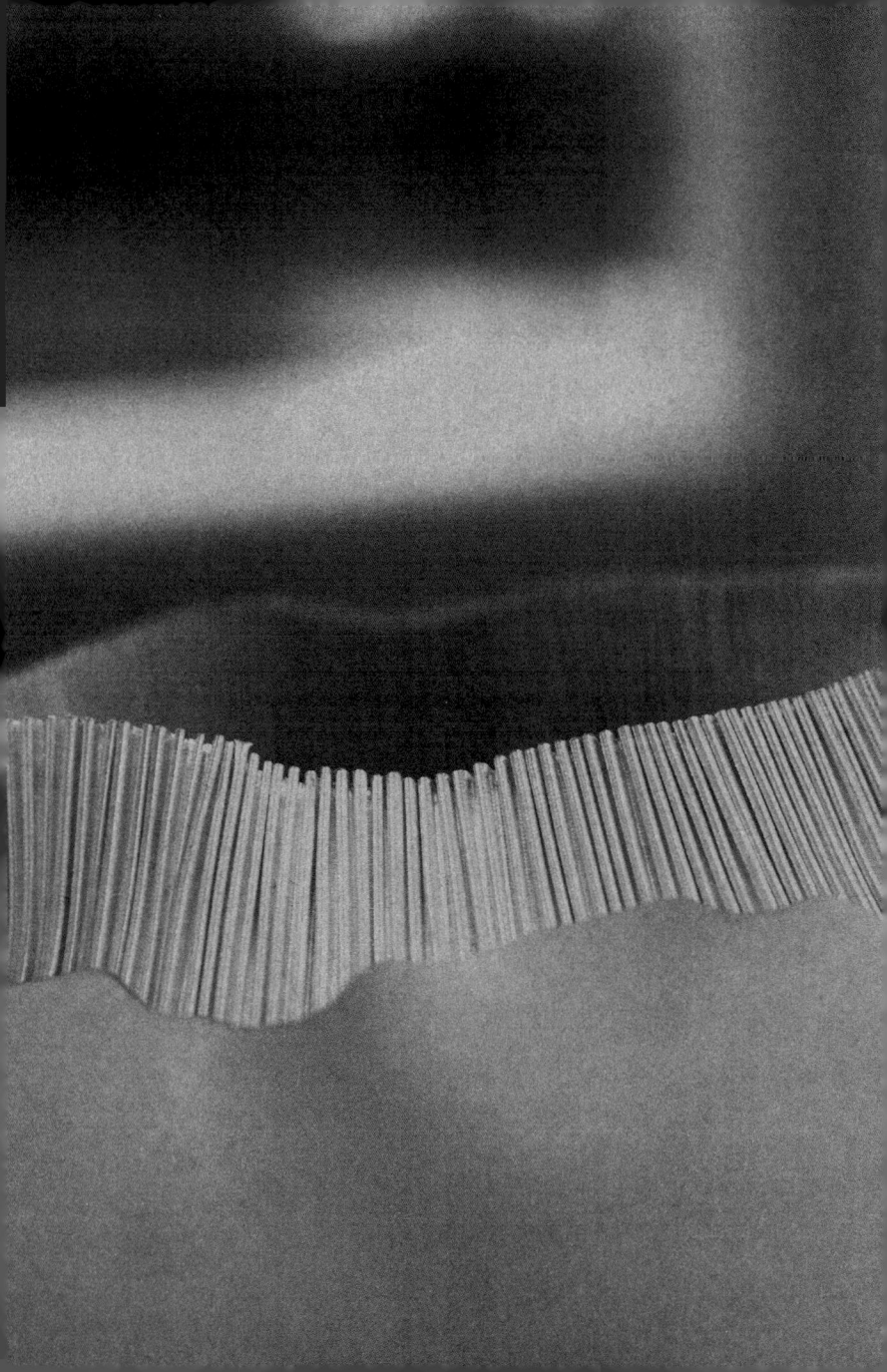

Ausstellungen / Exhibitions

Deutsches
Goldschmiedehaus
Hanau

DIVA
Museum voor Diamant,
Juwelen en Zilver,
Antwerpen

Schmuckmuseum
Pforzheim